Country Living

Cakes & Cupcakes

· COUNTRY BAKER ·

Cakes & Cupcakes

THE EDITORS OF
COUNTRY LIVING MAGAZINE

Foreword by Rachel Newman

Country Living

H E A R S T   B O O K S   ·   N E W   Y O R K

Photography Credits
Pages 17, 53, 71, 72, Richard Jeffery
Page 18, John Uher
Page 35, Dennis M. Gottlieb
Page 36, Charles Gold
Page 54, Victor Scocozza

•

•

It is the policy of William Morrow and Company, Inc., and its imprints and affiliates,
recognizing the importance of preserving what has been written, to print the books we
publish on acid-free paper, and we exert our best efforts to that end.

•

Library of Congress Cataloging-in-Publication Data
Country Living.
Country living, country baker. Cakes & cupcakes :
foreword by Rachel Newman. — 1st ed.
p. cm.
Includes index.
ISBN 0-688-12541-7 (alk. paper)
1. Cake. I. Country living (New York, N.Y.) II. Title.
III. Title: Country baker. IV. Title: Cakes & cupcakes.
V. Title: Cakes and cupcakes.
TX771.C64   1993
641.8'653—dc20   92-33221
                                                          CIP

•

Printed in Singapore
First Edition
2 3 4 5 6 7 8 9 10

•

Country Living Staff
Rachel Newman, *Editor-in-Chief*
Lucy Wing, *Contributing Food Editor*
Joanne Lamb Hayes, *Food Editor*
Elaine Van Dyne, *Associate Food Editor*

Produced by Smallwood and Stewart, Inc., New York City

Edited by Judith Blahnik
Designed by Tom Starace
Cover designed by Lynn Pieroni Fowler

Contents

Here is a collection of old-fashioned vegetable and spice cakes, shortcakes, and fruity upside-down cakes that remind us of our grandmothers. They might do the same for you.

Date Cake, Zucchini Fudge Cake, Caramel-Apple Spice Cake, Sour Cream Gingerbread, One-Two-Three-Four Cake, Cranberry Upside-Down Cake, Carrot Cake, Wild-Blueberry Cake, Real Strawberry Shortcakes, Pumpkin Shortcakes with Fall Fruit Filling, Red-Raspberry Torte

Although the airy, light angel food cake has been baked in the American oven for more than 100 years, the moist chiffon cake is relatively new, making its debut around 1940. Our favorites are all here.

Black-and-White Cake, Cocoa Chiffon Cream Cake, Lime Chiffon Cake, Chocolate Cream Roll, Marbled Mocha Angel Food Cake, Yellow Jelly-Roll Cake

From creamy cheesecake to delicate spice cake, this is a fine collection for special tastes and special occasions. They require a little extra time and effort, and they are all well worth it.

Fantastic Chokahlúa Cheesecake, Passionfruit Cheesecake, Cocoa Cake, Calico Spice Cake, Plaid Ribbon Cake, Stenciled Star Cake

Foreword

....

Which of us doesn't remember the thrill of seeing a birthday cake alight with candles, being carried into a darkened room? And who among us fails to be delighted and moved by the beauty of a wedding cake. It is this ritual of celebration that makes the cake, and its daintier counterpart the cupcake, such a well-loved treat.

From time to time at *Country Living* we ask our staff and their families to tell us their favorite foods. Inevitably, it seems, each list includes some sort of cake — accompanied, of course, by a tall glass of cold milk. When our food department sets out to develop recipes for these cakes, it usually takes several tries. Luckily for the staff the leftovers are placed on the giveaway table. Within minutes these cakes are reduced to a measly scattering of crumbs — and many of these are the cakes that were rejected!

To indulge in a sweet slice of cake is a luxury few of us can resist. If ever there was a treat that dieters saved themselves for, this is undoubtedly it. Let us eat cake!

Rachel Newman
Editor-in-Chief

Introduction

A HOUSE IS BEAUTIFUL NOT BECAUSE OF ITS
WALLS BUT BECAUSE OF ITS CAKES.

Russian proverb

Since the time that immigrating pioneers from all of Europe followed the lead of the first English settlers, American households have been enriched by a bounty of cakes from different cultures. Buttery English pound cakes, airy French cream-filled sponge cakes, cheesecakes from Italy, German bundled cakes, and Dutch chocolate-fudge layer cakes have all made their way more than once to the American table. Our collection of American classics celebrates this diversity. These recipes are our favorites — from traditional burnt-sugar checkerboard layer cake and simple one-bowl country confections to elaborate four-layer bake-sale winners and decorated birthday beauties. We've also included traditional homey loaves and tea cakes from our grandmothers' kitchens, as well as chocolate angel food, citrus chiffons, and cupcakes slathered with buttercream frosting.

What good bakers have known through the years is that the best way to ensure success with these classic cakes is to gather the freshest ingredients, combine them efficiently, and bake with the most reliable equipment one can find.

About The Ingredients

Our recipes require unsifted all-purpose, cake, or self-rising flour unless otherwise noted. We use fresh double-acting baking powder. Check the date on the can to make sure yours is fresh. If there is any doubt, stir 1 teaspoon into ½ cup hot water. A bubbling reaction means the baking powder is fresh.

Butter is lightly salted and always in the stick, as is margarine if you choose to use it. Don't substitute tub or whipped butter, or liquid or tub spread margarine. They contain more water and less fat than stick, and while they may be better for you on the dinner table, they are not better for your cakes: One of the secrets to light butter cakes and foam cakes is using the kind of fat called for in the recipe. Butter and margarine bring different flavors to the cake, but each has a fat content high enough to help leaven the cake.

The cocoa powder we use in our chocolate cakes is unsweetened, and when we call for chocolate squares, they are the 1-ounce squares found in bakers' chocolate. Eggs are always large and stored in their cartons in the refrigerator. Don't substitute unless noted in the recipe.

We recommend using real — not imitation — vanilla, maple, and almond extracts. The pungent flavor of the authentic extract permeates and perfumes your cake like no imitation can. Spices such as cinnamon, allspice, ginger, and cloves should be checked for freshness. If your jar or can is more than six months old, the spice may deliver disappointing results. Nutmeg is always best when freshly grated from the whole nutmeg. When we include walnuts, almonds, and pecans, they are in their natural unblanched state unless otherwise noted.

Some of our recipes call for liqueurs. Don't substitute a fruit juice for a liqueur unless it is suggested in the recipe. The acids in the juice could affect the action of the leaveners in the cake or dough.

About The Equipment

Give yourself enough space and time to assemble ingredients before you begin to mix. Three different-size mixing bowls and a set of metal dry measuring cups and glass liquid measuring cups are essential for stress-free baking.

Bake the cakes in the size pan or pans we suggest. Medium-weight restaurant-quality aluminum pans are the all-around best for good conduction of heat and even baking. Second best are ovenproof glass and ceramic. Nonstick metal pans are good for any cake except angel food and chiffon cakes. Buy bonded rather than sprayed-surface pans and grease and flour them in spite of their promises.

Baking Pans

These are the pans we find most useful and recommend that the home baker have at home:

Loaf pans: 5¾ by 3¼ inches
9 by 5 by 3 inches
8½ by 4½ inches
10-inch tube pan (preferably with a removable bottom)
10-inch decorative tube pan like a bundt pan or other fluted pan
9- and 10-inch round cake pans at least 1½ inches deep
9-inch springform pan
15½- by 10½-inch jelly-roll pan
1-cup decorative molds for individual cakes

A wire or wooden cooling rack is essential. The cake must cool evenly on a surface that allows air to circulate, preventing the bottom of the cake from becoming soggy. Buy a rack large enough to cool three 8-inch round cakes at once or use three small racks.

For decorating cakes with birthday messages and scalloped borders, we use a pastry bag with assorted tips. Washable nylon and disposable plastic are fine choices.

About The Method

For the purpose of saving space, we haven't described certain techniques in detail. When the recipe says "cool completely on a wire rack," it means to cool the cake to room temperature. When the recipe directs you to "unmold the cake," it means to loosen the edges with a sharp knife or metal spatula, invert the pan over a plate, gently shake the pan until the cake comes loose on the plate, then invert the plate and place the cake right side up on a wire cooling rack or serving plate. And when making cupcakes, "divide the batter among the prepared muffin-pan cups" means to fill each, using a ladle or spouted cup, two thirds full.

Almond Fruitcakes

....

These delightful loaves are spirited with rum and packed with fruit and nuts. The added egg whites make them lighter than most fruitcakes.

MAKES 3 SMALL LOAVES, OR 12 SERVINGS

1 12-ounce package diced mixed dried fruit
⅓ cup light rum or dry sherry
2 cups sifted cake flour
¾ cup sugar
1 teaspoon baking powder
¼ teaspoon salt
1 cup slivered blanched almonds, toasted

½ cup (1 stick) butter or margarine, melted
1 teaspoon vanilla extract
6 egg whites, at room temperature
18 whole blanched almonds (optional)
¼ cup light corn syrup for glazing (optional)

1. In a small bowl, combine the dried fruit with the rum; let the mixture stand 1 hour. Meanwhile, grease and flour three 5¾- by 3¼-inch loaf pans. Heat the oven to 325°F.

2. In a large bowl, combine the flour, ½ cup sugar, the baking powder, and salt. Stir in the fruit-rum mixture until the fruit is coated with the flour mixture. Stir in the slivered almonds, butter, and vanilla.

3. In a large bowl, with an electric mixer on high speed, beat the egg whites until foamy. Gradually beat in the remaining ¼ cup sugar until stiff peaks form. Fold the egg whites, one third at a time, into the flour mixture. Divide the batter among the prepared pans. If desired, arrange 6 whole almonds on the batter in each pan.

4. Bake the cakes 1 hour, or until a cake tester inserted in the center comes out clean. Cool the cakes in the pans on wire racks for 10 minutes. Remove the cakes from the pans and cool completely on the racks.

5. To glaze the cakes, if desired, heat the corn syrup to boiling; brush the syrup on the cakes and let them stand until the glaze dries. Wrap the cakes with plastic wrap and store them overnight before slicing.

Glazed Devil's Food Cake

....

Ｆor the classic chocolate cake lover only, these chocolate layers, divid-
ed by rich chocolate frosting and burnished to a smooth finish with
a chocolate glaze, provide a triple treat.

MAKES 12 SERVINGS

¾ cup (1½ sticks) butter or
   margarine, softened
1½ cups granulated sugar
¾ teaspoon salt
1 tablespoon vanilla extract
3½ cups cake flour
¾ cup cocoa powder
2 teaspoons baking soda
2½ cups water
4 egg whites, at room
   temperature

Cocoa Frosting:
⅓ cup butter or margarine,
   softened

1½ pounds confectioners'
   sugar
⅓ cup cocoa powder
1 teaspoon ground cinnamon
¾ teaspoon vanilla extract
⅓ to ½ cup milk

Chocolate Glaze:
6 1-ounce squares semisweet
   chocolate
¼ cup (½ stick) butter
3 tablespoons cold water
¾ cup confectioners' sugar

1. Heat the oven to 350°F. Generously grease and flour three 9-inch
round baking pans. In a large bowl, with an electric mixer on medium
speed, beat the butter, ¾ cup granulated sugar, the salt, and vanilla until
the mixture is fluffy.

2. In a large sifter, combine the flour, cocoa, and baking soda. Sift
the flour mixture over the butter mixture; add the water. With the
mixer on low speed, beat the mixture just until smooth.

3. In a medium-size bowl, with clean beaters and the mixer on high
speed, beat the egg whites until soft peaks form. Gradually add the
remaining ¾ cup granulated sugar and continue to beat until stiff peaks
form. Fold the egg whites, one third at a time, into the batter. Divide
the batter among the prepared pans.

4. Bake the cakes 20 to 25 minutes, or until a cake tester inserted in
the center comes out clean. Cool the cakes in the pans on wire racks for

10 minutes. Remove the cakes from the pans and cool completely on the wire racks.

5. Prepare the Cocoa Frosting: In a medium-size bowl, with the mixer on medium speed, beat the butter, confectioners' sugar, cocoa, cinnamon, vanilla, and milk until smooth. Set aside.

6. To assemble the cake, place one cake layer on a cardboard round cut exactly to fit the layer. Spread the top with ⅓ cup frosting. Place a second cake layer on top of the first, and spread the top with ⅓ cup frosting. Top with the remaining cake layer. Spread a thin, smooth layer of frosting over the top and side of the cake. Refrigerate for 1 hour.

7. Prepare the Chocolate Glaze: In the top of a double boiler, over hot (not boiling) water, melt the chocolate and butter. Stir in the cold water and confectioners' sugar until smooth.

8. Place the chilled cake on a wire rack with a tray or baking sheet underneath it. Spoon the glaze over the top of the cake. Spread evenly, allowing the glaze to run down the side of the cake. Gently smooth the glaze to evenly coat the side of the cake. Refrigerate the cake, on the rack over the tray, until the glaze is firm, about 1 hour. Using two pancake turners, place the cake on a serving plate.

CUTTING THE CAKE

Delicate cakes, like sponge, chiffon, and angel food, must be cut slowly and gently with a wire cake break or a serrated knife. Layered butter cakes should be cut with a sharp, thin-blade knife. Cakes with soft, fluffy butter frostings and egg-white frostings and all cheesecakes will stick to the knife unless you wipe it clean with a hot, damp cloth or sponge after each cut.

Sheet and pan cakes are usually cut into squares with a long knife and lifted from the pan with the help of a metal spatula. Cut round layer cakes into wedges beginning with the tip of the knife at the center of the cake, and use a spatula for lifting the cake wedge to a plate. Slice fruitcakes very thin and clean the knife after each cut.

Old-Time Spice Cake

The search for spices is what lead Columbus to the shores of America and almost everything he was looking for is in this cake — nutmeg, cloves, and cinnamon. Whole nutmeg freshly ground with a grater is much more potent and flavorful than the packaged ground spice.

MAKES 10 SERVINGS

¾ cup (1½ sticks) butter or margarine, softened
¾ cup firmly packed light-brown sugar
2 eggs
1 10¾-ounce can condensed tomato soup, undiluted
2 cups all-purpose flour
2 teaspoons baking powder
1 teaspoon ground cinnamon
½ teaspoon baking soda
½ teaspoon ground nutmeg

¼ teaspoon ground cloves
⅓ cup milk
½ cup chopped pecans
½ cup dark seedless raisins

Cream Cheese Frosting (page 52)

¼ cup dark seedless raisins for decoration (optional)
¼ cup pecan halves for decoration (optional)

1. Heat the oven to 350°F. Grease and flour two 8-inch round baking pans. In a medium-size bowl, with an electric mixer on medium speed, beat the butter and sugar until fluffy. Add the eggs, one at a time, beating well after each addition. Beat in the soup until well combined.

2. In a small bowl, combine the flour, baking powder, cinnamon, baking soda, nutmeg, and cloves. With the mixer on low speed and beginning and ending with the flour mixture, alternately beat the flour mixture and the milk mixture into the soup mixture until well combined. Fold in the chopped pecans and raisins. Divide the batter between the prepared pans.

3. Bake the cakes 25 to 30 minutes, or until a cake tester inserted in the center comes out clean. Cool the cakes in the pans on wire racks for 10 minutes. Remove the cakes from the pans and cool completely on the wire racks.

4. Prepare the Cream Cheese Frosting.

5. To assemble the cake, place one cake layer on a serving plate. Spread the top with ⅓ cup of the cream cheese frosting. Place the other cake layer on top of the first. Spread the top and side of the cake with the remaining frosting. If desired, arrange the raisins and pecans on top in 2 concentric circles.

T I P S   F O R   S U C C E S S F U L   C A K E S

Cake baking is fun, and you are rewarded with a beautiful, delicious cake as well. Follow a few golden rules of baking, and you won't be disappointed. Assemble all ingredients and equipment before you begin so that you can move from one step to the next easily and without too much time elapsing.

Measure dry ingredients using metal dry-measure cups and spoons and the dip, scoop, and level method: Dip the spoon or cup into the flour or sugar and scoop so that the measuring cup is over-flowing. Then, with a metal spatula or knife, level the measure off.

Be sure to cream the butter with the sugar until light and fluffy. This traps air bubbles and ensures your cake will rise well. Follow the directions that call for adding dry and liquid ingredients alternately. The point is to create a smooth batter without loosing air bubbles; adding flour last binds all the ingredients together.

Grease and flour the cake pan very well. Apply a thin coat of vegetable shortening or butter to the inner surface of the pan. Sprinkle with flour, tapping the pan until all the greased surface is lightly coated with flour. For extra insurance, cut a round of waxed paper to fit the bottom of the pan and place it in the prepared pan. Then grease and flour the waxed paper.

Bunt Cake

Though we spell it the way it is pronounced, this cake is named for the German word bund (meaning "bundle"). The dense, round butter cake introduced to the Midwest by German immigrants early in the century became the rage in the 60s after one took first prize in the Pillsbury Bake-Off. Grease the intricate fluted Bundt pan thoroughly, and use a vegetable spray if necessary.

MAKES 12 SERVINGS

4 eggs, separated, at room
    temperature
2 cups confectioners' sugar
¾ cup (1½ sticks) butter,
    softened
1 tablespoon grated lemon
    rind
3 cups cake flour

1 tablespoon baking powder
½ teaspoon salt
1¼ cups milk
2 teaspoons granulated sugar

Confectioners' sugar
    (optional)

1. Heat the oven to 350°F. Grease and flour a 9-inch Bundt pan. In a large bowl, with an electric mixer on high speed, beat the egg whites until stiff peaks form; set aside.

2. In another large bowl, with the same beaters and the mixer on medium speed, beat 2 cups confectioners' sugar and the butter until the mixture forms a smooth paste. Add the egg yolks and lemon rind; beat until the mixture is thick and lemon colored, about 3 minutes.

3. In a medium-size bowl, combine the flour, baking powder, and salt. With the mixer on low speed, and beginning and ending with the flour mixture, alternately beat the flour mixture and the milk into the sugar mixture until well combined. Gently fold the egg whites into the batter. Spoon the batter into the prepared pan; sprinkle with the granulated sugar.

4. Bake the cake 1 hour, or until a cake tester inserted in the center comes out clean. Cool the cake in the pan on a wire rack for 5 minutes. Remove the pan and cool the cake completely on the rack. Place the cake on a serving plate, and if desired, sift confectioners' sugar over the top before serving.

Lane Cake, page 22

Dad's Wacky Cake, Page 31

Elegant Strawberry Shortcake

This cake has an easy elegance, and for as long as we can remember it has been America's favorite to enjoy at summer picnics. It tastes best at room temperature, right after assembling, but can (and must) be refrigerated until ready to serve.

MAKES 10 SERVINGS

2½ cups cake flour
1 cup granulated sugar
2½ teaspoons baking
  powder
½ teaspoon salt
¾ cup (1½ sticks) butter or
  margarine, softened

1 cup milk
3 eggs
1½ teaspoons vanilla extract
2 pint baskets (4 cups)
  strawberries
2 cups (1 pint) heavy cream
¼ cup confectioners' sugar

1. Heat the oven to 350°F. Grease and flour two 9-inch round baking pans. In a large bowl, combine the flour, granulated sugar, baking powder, and salt. Add the butter, milk, eggs, and 1 teaspoon vanilla. With an electric mixer on medium speed, beat the batter, scraping the bowl frequently, just until smooth. Divide the batter between the prepared pans and smooth the tops.

2. Bake the cakes 30 to 35 minutes, or until a cake tester inserted in the center comes out clean. Cool the cakes in the pans on wire racks for 5 minutes, remove from the pans, and cool completely on the racks.

3. Rinse and hull the strawberries. Set them aside on paper towels to drain. In a medium-size bowl, with the mixer on medium speed, beat the cream, confectioners' sugar, and the remaining ½ teaspoon vanilla until stiff peaks form.

4. To assemble the cake, place one cake layer, upside down, on a serving plate. Spread the top with 1 cup whipped cream. Slice enough strawberries in half to make ⅔ cup and arrange on the whipped cream.

5. Top the whipped cream and strawberries with the remaining cake layer, right side up. Spread the top and side of the cake with the remaining whipped cream. Slice the remaining strawberries in half; press them, cut side down, into the whipped cream on the top; and make a border at the bottom of the cake.

Burnt-Sugar Checkerboard Cake

The colors of dark caramel and deep chocolate in a checkerboard pattern made this layer cake a favorite at American soda fountains, bake sales, and county fairs. For ensured success, use a checkerboard cake divider set, which is available in many housewares stores.

MAKES 12 SERVINGS

2½ cups granulated sugar
1 cup boiling water
1 teaspoon lemon juice
4 cups all-purpose flour
1 tablespoon baking powder
½ teaspoon salt
½ to 1 cup milk
1½ cups (3 sticks) butter or
   margarine, softened
4 eggs
2 teaspoons vanilla extract

6 1-ounce squares semisweet
   chocolate, melted

Mocha Frosting:
1 cup (2 sticks) butter or
   margarine, softened
½ cup vegetable shortening
2 tablespoons cocoa powder
2 tablespoons cold coffee
2 teaspoons vanilla extract
2 cups confectioners' sugar

1. In a 2-quart saucepan, heat 1½ cups granulated sugar, ¼ cup boiling water, and the lemon juice to boiling over high heat. Reduce the heat to medium, and cook until the mixture is a dark, golden brown, 14 to 16 minutes. Let the mixture cool 1 minute; carefully stir in the remaining ¾ cup boiling water. Pour the burnt-sugar mixture into a 2-cup measuring cup; set aside to cool to room temperature.

2. Grease and flour three 9-inch round baking pans of a checkerboard cake set. Generously grease the checkerboard divider. Heat the oven to 350°F. In a medium-size bowl, combine the flour, baking powder, and salt. Add enough milk to the cooled burnt-sugar mixture in the measuring cup to measure 2 cups.

3. In a large bowl, with an electric mixer on medium speed, beat the butter and the remaining 1 cup granulated sugar until light and fluffy. Add the eggs, one at a time, beating well after each addition. Beat in the vanilla. Reduce the mixer speed to low. Beginning and ending with the flour mixture, alternately beat the flour mixture and the burnt-sugar-milk mixture into the butter mixture until well combined.

4. Transfer 3½ cups batter to a medium-size bowl; stir in the melted chocolate until the mixture is well combined. Place the well-greased checkerboard divider into one prepared cake pan. Fill the center and outer circles half full with burnt-sugar batter; fill the middle circle half full with chocolate batter. Carefully lift the divider out of the batter. Repeat the process in another prepared cake pan. Clean and re-grease the divider. In the third pan, fill the center and outer circles with the remaining chocolate batter and the middle circle with the remaining burnt-sugar batter.

5. Bake the cakes 30 to 35 minutes, or until a cake tester inserted in the center comes out clean. Cool the cakes in the pans on wire racks for 10 minutes. Remove the cakes from the pans and cool them completely on the racks.

6. Prepare the Mocha Frosting: In a large bowl, with the mixer on medium speed, beat the butter and the shortening until light and fluffy. Reduce the mixer speed to low and beat in the cocoa, coffee, and vanilla until well combined. Gradually beat in the confectioners' sugar until the frosting is creamy and smooth.

7. To assemble the cake, place one cake layer with a burnt-sugar center on a serving plate. Spread the top with ⅓ cup frosting. Place the cake layer with the chocolate center on top of the first layer. Spread the top with ⅓ cup frosting. Top with the remaining cake layer. Spread the top and side of the cake with the remaining frosting.

UNEVEN LAYERS

If the cake layer isn't level across the top, you will most likely not have an even-looking finished cake. To even the top, allow the cake to cool completely on a rack. Replace it in the baking pan and using the rim as a guide, run a long serrated knife across the top of the cake, until the cake is level with the rim.

Lane Cake
PHOTOGRAPH ON PAGE 17

Probably the South's most famous Christmas cake, this is credited to Emma Rylander Lane of Clayton, Alabama, who won a prize with it at the Georgia state fair. Three cake layers are spread with a creamy filling of coconut, citrus, dried fruits, and pecans and the cake is topped with whipped cream.

MAKES 12 SERVINGS

Coconut Pecan Filling:
1 cup granulated sugar
½ cup (1 stick) butter
½ cup orange juice
1 tablespoon grated orange rind
8 egg yolks, beaten (reserve the whites for cake batter)
1 cup chopped pecans
½ cup chopped candied cherries
1 cup shredded unsweetened coconut

8 egg whites, at room temperature
2 cups granulated sugar
1 cup (2 sticks) butter, softened
1 tablespoon vanilla extract
3½ cups cake flour
1 tablespoon baking powder
½ teaspoon salt
1¼ cups milk

Whipped Cream Frosting:
2 cups (1 pint) heavy cream
2 tablespoons confectioners' sugar

1. Prepare the Coconut Pecan Filling: In the top of a double boiler over simmering water, combine the granulated sugar, butter, orange juice, and orange rind. Stir the mixture occasionally until the butter melts and the sugar dissolves. Spoon 2 tablespoons of the hot sugar mixture into the egg yolks, stirring constantly. Pour the egg yolk mixture into the remaining sugar mixture and continue to cook, stirring constantly, until the mixture thickens to a pudding — about 20 minutes. Remove from the heat. Reserve 1 tablespoon each of the chopped pecans and candied cherries; stir the remaining pecans, cherries, and coconut into the filling. Cool to room temperature; cover and refrigerate.

2. Heat the oven to 325°F. Grease and flour three 9-inch round baking pans. In a large bowl, with an electric mixer on high speed, beat the

egg whites until foamy; add ¼ cup granulated sugar and beat until stiff peaks form. Set aside.

3. In another large bowl, with the same beaters and the mixer on medium speed, beat the butter and the remaining 1¾ cups granulated sugar until the mixture is light and fluffy. Add the vanilla and mix until well blended. In a medium-size bowl, combine the flour, baking powder, and salt. With the mixer on low speed and beginning and ending with the flour mixture, alternately beat the flour mixture and the milk into the sugar mixture until a smooth batter forms. Gently fold the egg whites into the batter. Divide the batter among the prepared pans.

4. Bake the cakes 30 to 35 minutes, or until a cake tester inserted in the center comes out clean. Cool the cakes in the pans on wire racks for 10 minutes. Remove the cakes from the pans and cool completely on the racks. Trim the tops of the layers to make them level, if necessary.

5. Prepare the Whipped Cream Frosting: In a large bowl, with the mixer on medium speed, beat the cream and confectioners' sugar until stiff peaks form. Place one cake layer on a serving plate and spread the top with half the filling. Place a second cake layer on top of the first; spread the top with the remaining filling. Top with the remaining cake layer. Spread the top and side of the cake with the whipped cream frosting. Garnish the top with the reserved pecans and cherries. Serve the cake immediately, or refrigerate for later.

UNMOLDING THE CAKE

Run a knife or long metal spatula around the edge of the cake. With a towel or potholder, hold the pan upside down and give it a firm jerk to free the cake. When the cake falls onto the rack, carefully invert it so it is top side up. Don't leave it upside down on the rack or you will have parallel rack marks across the top of your cake. Be sure the cake is cooled before frosting; it can take one or two hours to cool completely.

Chocolate-Coconut Cake

....

There is no substitute for the taste and texture of fresh coconut, and marrying coconut and chocolate creates a wonderful flavor combination. Choose a heavy coconut with brown skin and the sound of liquid splashing inside when you shake it. (Stale ones will have very little liquid.) Freshly grated coconut meat will last up to 5 days, covered tightly and stored in the refrigerator.

MAKES 10 SERVINGS

1 cup (2 sticks) butter, softened
1¾ cups sugar
1 tablespoon vanilla extract
3 eggs
2¼ cups cake flour
1 cup cocoa powder
1½ teaspoons baking powder
1 teaspoon baking soda
¼ teaspoon salt
1¾ cups milk
1 fresh coconut

Seven-Minute Frosting:
3 egg whites, at room temperature
2¼ cups sugar
Reserved coconut liquid
2 tablespoons light corn syrup
⅛ teaspoon salt
¼ teaspoon coconut flavoring, or ½ teaspoon vanilla extract

1. Heat the oven to 350°F. Grease three 9-inch round baking pans. In a large bowl, with an electric mixer on medium speed, beat the butter, 1¾ cups sugar, and vanilla until light and fluffy. Add the eggs, one at a time, beating well after each addition.

2. Into a medium-size bowl, sift the flour, cocoa, baking powder, baking soda, and salt. With the mixer on low speed, and beginning and ending with the flour mixture, alternately beat the flour mixture and the milk into the butter mixture just until well combined. Divide the batter among the prepared pans.

3. Bake the cakes 25 to 30 minutes, or until a cake tester inserted in the center comes out clean. Cool the cakes in the pans on wire racks for 10 minutes. Remove the cakes from the pans and cool completely on the racks.

4. Meanwhile, with an ice pick, pierce holes in the eyes of the coconut; drain the liquid into a measuring cup. Add enough water to make ½ cup coconut liquid and reserve for the frosting. Wrap the coconut in a towel and strike it with a hammer until the coconut breaks into 3 or 4 pieces. With a sharp knife or screwdriver, pry the coconut meat from the shell and peel off the dark skin. With a grater, shred the coconut meat into a bowl. Cover the bowl with plastic wrap and set aside.

5. Prepare the Seven-Minute Frosting: In the top of a double boiler, combine the egg whites, sugar, the reserved coconut liquid, the corn syrup, and salt. With a hand-held or portable electric mixer on high speed, beat the mixture over boiling water until stiff peaks form, about 7 minutes. Remove the mixture from the heat. Add the coconut flavoring, and continue beating until the frosting is thick, about 2 minutes longer.

6. To assemble the cake, place one cake layer on a serving plate. Spread the top with ⅓ cup frosting; sprinkle with ⅓ cup shredded coconut. Place a second cake layer on top of the first. Spread the top with ⅓ cup frosting; sprinkle with ⅓ cup shredded coconut. Top with the remaining cake layer. Spread the top and side of the cake with the remaining frosting. Sprinkle the top with shredded coconut, and pat some on the side of the cake.

H O W   T O   C R A C K   A   C O C O N U T

One proven method for cracking a coconut is simply to throw it hard against rock, pavement, or cement. It will usually break into 3 or more pieces. A more convenient method might be using your microwave. Pierce the eyes of the coconut with an ice pick and drain the liquid. Wrap the coconut in plastic wrap and microwave on high for 5 minutes. It will be very hot. Let it stand 15 minutes, then wrap it in a towel and split it by giving it 2 or 3 hard whacks with a hammer. Pry it open with screwdriver, and dig out the white meat. Peel off the dark skin. You can also warm the coconut in a 450°F oven for 20 minutes, wrap it in a towel, and hit with a hammer.

Checkerboard Chocolate Cake

Here is a simple one-layer cake with a rich, dark glaze. The confectioners' sugar checkerboard design gives it a stylish look which makes it perfect for a dessert buffet. Create a checkerboard pattern on brown paper: With a ruler and pencil, draw and cut out a 10-inch square. Draw 9 horizontal and 9 vertical lines, dividing the square into one hundred 1-inch squares. Make an X in every other box, checkerboard fashion. With a matte knife or single-edge razor blade, cut out each box marked X (they form diagonal rows), leaving enough paper at the points to connect the boxes.

MAKES 10 SERVINGS

1 cup boiling water
¾ cup cocoa powder
1½ cups granulated sugar
¾ cup (1½ sticks) butter,
    softened
4 eggs
2 teaspoons vanilla extract
2 cups cake flour
1 teaspoon baking powder
½ teaspoon baking soda
½ teaspoon salt

Chocolate Glaze:
2 tablespoons heavy cream
1½ 1-ounce squares
    semisweet chocolate,
    finely chopped

Paper checkerboard pattern
    (optional)

Confectioners' sugar
    (optional)

1. In a small bowl, combine the boiling water and cocoa; stir until the cocoa dissolves and the mixture is blended. Set aside to cool. Grease a 10-inch round baking pan. Line the bottom with waxed paper; grease and flour the waxed paper.

2. In a large bowl, with an electric mixer on medium speed, beat the granulated sugar and butter until light and fluffy. Add the eggs, one at a time, beating well after each addition. Beat in the vanilla.

3. When the cocoa mixture has cooled completely, heat the oven to 350°F. In a medium-size bowl, combine the flour, baking powder, baking soda, and salt. With the mixer on low speed, add the flour mixture to the butter mixture in 2 batches, beating until the batter is smooth. Stir the cocoa mixture into the batter until well blended. Pour the batter into the prepared pan.

4. Bake the cake 55 to 60 minutes, or until a cake tester inserted in the center comes out clean. Cool the cake in the pan on a wire rack for 10 minutes. Invert the pan, unmold the cake, and remove the waxed paper. Place the cake, right side up, on the rack to cool completely.

5. Prepare the Chocolate Glaze: In a small saucepan, heat the cream to boiling. Remove from the heat. Add the chocolate; stir until the chocolate is completely melted and the mixture is well blended. Set aside to thicken and cool slightly.

6. Place the rack holding the cake on a baking sheet or tray. Spread the chocolate glaze evenly over the top of the cake. If stenciling the cake with the checkerboard pattern, allow the glaze to dry completely. To stencil the checkerboard, place the paper pattern on the cake, allowing the chocolate glaze to show through; if necessary, fasten the corners with toothpicks. Sift confectioners' sugar over the cake to coat lightly. Carefully remove the stencil. Using two pancake turners, place the cake on a serving plate.

DECORATING THE CAKE

Any plain frosted cake can be given special character with a little effort. Dragées, for example, are tiny silver and gold balls of sugar that can be arranged in a pattern on top of a cake. They are inexpensive and quick to use.

Create chocolate curls by shaving a chocolate bar with a vegetable peeler or sprinkle ground nuts or sliced almonds over a cake. Pipe a border of a contrasting color frosting in stars or scallops around the top or bottom of the cake to make a frosted cake look elegant.

Make a stencil of autumn leaves, stars, spirals, checkerboards, or starbursts or use an alphabet stencil to turn a plain cake into a personal one. Place the stencil on the cake as directed in our Stenciled Star Cake, page 84, and dust with confectioners' sugar.

Boston Cream Pie

In 1886, the Boston Cooking School cookbook published a recipe for Cream Pie, which was a simple layer cake filled with light cream and dusted with sugar. One hundred years of improvisation have led to several versions of this recipe. Ours is a very light chiffon cake with cream filling and a semisweet chocolate glaze.

MAKES 10 SERVINGS

2 cups cake flour	Cream Filling:
1 cup sugar	1½ cups milk
2½ teaspoons baking powder	2 tablespoons cornstarch
½ teaspoon salt	¼ cup sugar
2 eggs, separated, at room temperature	1 egg
	1 tablespoon vanilla extract
⅓ cup vegetable oil	
¾ cup milk	Chocolate Glaze:
2 teaspoons vanilla extract	¼ cup water
	2 tablespoons sugar
	½ cup (3 ounces) semisweet chocolate chips

1. Heat the oven to 350°F. Grease and flour two 9-inch round baking pans. In a large bowl, combine the flour, ¾ cup sugar, the baking powder, and salt; set aside.

2. In a small bowl, with an electric mixer on high speed, beat the egg whites until soft peaks form. Very gradually beat in the remaining ¼ cup sugar until stiff peaks form. Set aside.

3. Add the egg yolks, oil, and ½ cup milk to the flour mixture. With the mixer on medium speed, beat the flour mixture, scraping the bowl occasionally, until smooth. Add the remaining ¼ cup milk and the vanilla. Beat just until the ingredients are combined. Gently fold the egg whites into the batter. Divide the batter between the prepared pans.

4. Bake the cakes 20 to 25 minutes, or until a cake tester inserted in the center comes out clean. Cool the cakes in the pans on wire racks for 5 minutes. Remove the cakes from the pans and cool on the racks.

5. Prepare the Cream Filling: In a small bowl, combine ½ cup milk, the cornstarch, ¼ cup sugar, egg, and vanilla; stir until blended. In a 1-quart saucepan, heat the remaining 1 cup milk to boiling.

6. When the milk just reaches boiling, with a wire whisk, gradually stir in the cornstarch mixture. Heat to boiling, stirring constantly. Reduce the heat and simmer, stirring constantly for 1 minute. Transfer the filling to a 1-quart bowl. Cover the surface of the filling with plastic wrap to prevent a skin from forming and set aside to cool to room temperature.

7. Prepare the Chocolate Glaze: In a 1-quart saucepan, heat the water and sugar to boiling. Add the chocolate chips; stir the glaze until smooth. Cool the glaze 10 to 15 minutes, or until it is slightly thickened.

8. To assemble the cake, place one cake layer, upside down, on a serving plate. Spread the top with the cream filling. Top with the remaining cake layer, right side up. Spoon the glaze over the top; spread just to the edge of the cake. Serve immediately, or refrigerate until ready to serve. Refrigerate any remaining cake.

PASTRY BAG

It's great fun to turn a simple layer cake into a decorated birthday, anniversary, or celebration cake, and a pastry bag is an invaluable tool. Buy an assortment of tips and choose a medium- to large-size bag. Cloth, nylon, and even disposable plastic are all easily available at most cookware shops. To prepare the bag for use, drop a tip into the bag and slide it down to the small opening of the bag. Twist the bag and tuck some of the twisted bag into the tip itself to fix the tip in place. To fill the bag, fold about half the bag down to form a cuff on the outside over your hand. With a spatula, scoop the cream or frosting into the bag until the bag is about two-thirds full. Unfold the cuff and twist the wide end together to push all the air out of the bag. Hold the twisted end in one hand and push down toward the tip with the other hand to get the filling flowing. Practice creating designs and writing messages on plates, baking sheets, and even pieces of waxed paper.

Doily Cake

PHOTOGRAPH ON PAGE 35

Moist and spicy, this one-pan cake is surprisingly delicious — fast enough for afternoon coffee or an after-school snack, and pretty enough for a fancy dessert buffet. Use an 8-inch round paper doily to stencil the decorative top, securing it with toothpicks. Dust with confectioners' sugar in a breeze-free part of the house.

MAKES 9 SERVINGS

1½ cups granulated sugar
1 cup (2 sticks) butter or margarine, softened
2 eggs
2½ cups all-purpose flour
2 teaspoons baking soda
2 teaspoons ground cinnamon
1 teaspoon ground cloves
½ teaspoon salt

¼ teaspoon ground nutmeg
2 cups unsweetened apple-sauce
1 cup dark seedless raisins
1 cup coarsely chopped walnuts
2 tablespoons confectioners' sugar

1. Heat the oven to 350°F. Grease and flour a 9-inch square baking pan. In a large bowl, with an electric mixer on medium speed, beat the granulated sugar and butter until light and fluffy. Add the eggs, one at a time, beating well after each addition

2. In a medium-size bowl, combine the flour, baking soda, cinnamon, cloves, salt, and nutmeg. With the mixer on low and beginning and ending with the flour mixture, alternately beat the flour mixture and the applesauce into the butter mixture. Stir in the raisins and walnuts. Spread the batter evenly in the prepared pan.

3. Bake the cake 50 to 55 minutes, or until a cake tester inserted in the center comes out clean. Cool the cake in the pan on a wire rack for 10 minutes. Remove the cake from the pan and cool completely on the rack.

4. Just before serving, place a paper doily or other cake stencil on the cake. Sift the confectioners' sugar over the cake. Carefully remove the doily. Using two spatulas, place the cake on a serving plate. To serve, cut the cake into squares.

Dad's Wacky Cake

PHOTOGRAPH ON PAGE 18

The King Arthur Flour Company originally published this recipe and unless you're familiar with the fad "dump" cakes that were the rage years ago, you'll doubt that a good-tasting cake can and does emerge here. Simply combine all the ingredients right in the baking pan; stir and bake. It's wacky, but try it!

MAKES 6 SERVINGS

1½ cups all-purpose flour
1 cup sugar
3 tablespoons cocoa powder
1 teaspoon baking powder
1 teaspoon baking soda
½ teaspoon salt
5 tablespoons butter, melted

1 tablespoon distilled white
   vinegar
1 teaspoon vanilla extract
1 cup cold water
1 cup semisweet chocolate
   minichips
Vanilla ice cream (optional)

1. Heat the oven to 350°F. Sift the flour, sugar, cocoa, baking powder, baking soda, and salt into a 10- by 7-inch, 8-inch square, or 9-inch square baking pan. With your index finger, make 3 holes in the flour mixture. Pour the butter into one hole, the vinegar into another hole, and the vanilla into the remaining hole. Pour the cold water over all. Stir the mixture until well combined.

2. Bake the cake 25 to 35 minutes or until a cake tester inserted in the center comes out clean. Immediately top the cake with the chocolate chips. Bake the cake 2 to 3 minutes longer, or just until the chips soften.

3. With a spatula, spread the softened chocolate chips evenly over the top of the cake. Cool the cake completely in the pan on a wire rack. Cut the cake into squares, and serve with vanilla ice cream, if desired.

COOLING TIP

To prevent cakes from sticking to the wire rack, grease the rack lightly before placing the cakes to cool.

Whipped Cream Pound Cake

Before the invention of baking powder, the only leaveners that could ensure a light, palatable cake were eggs, butter, and elbow grease. A baker would have to beat a long time to get enough air into the batter. This cake has a traditional Colonial taste and texture without baking powder, thanks to the modern electric mixer.

MAKES 12 SERVINGS

1 cup (2 sticks) butter, softened	*3 cups all-purpose flour*
2 cups sugar	*1 cup (½ pint) heavy cream*
6 eggs	*1 teaspoon vanilla extract*

1. Heat the oven to 325°F. Grease and flour a 10-inch Bundt or tube pan. In a large bowl, with an electric mixer on medium speed, beat the butter and sugar until light and fluffy. Add the eggs, one at a time, beating well after each addition.

2. Reduce the mixer speed to low, and beginning and ending with the flour, alternately beat the flour and the cream into the butter mixture, beating well after each addition, until well combined. Beat in the vanilla. Pour the batter into the prepared pan.

3. Bake the cake 60 to 75 minutes, or until a cake tester inserted in the center comes out clean. Cool the cake in the pan on a wire rack for 10 minutes. Remove the cake from the pan, and cool completely on the rack. Place the cake on a serving plate.

COOLING

Cool most cakes on a rack 10 minutes. Then remove the cake from the pan and let it cool right side up on a wire rack. All airy cakes that are made without shortening or fat such as angel food and chiffon cakes should be cooled upside down in the tube pan to keep them from falling.

Honey Cakes

Honey and a splash of orange juice give these sweet loaves a golden color and a light citrus flavor. These cakes travel well and are perfect for picnic dessert and pot lucks, or slice and serve them at home for breakfast, warmed and slathered with butter.

MAKES 16 SERVINGS

3 eggs	1½ teaspoons grated orange
¾ cup honey	rind
¾ cup sugar	2⅔ cups all-purpose flour
⅓ cup vegetable oil	¾ teaspoon baking powder
3 tablespoons orange juice	¾ teaspoon baking soda
1½ tablespoons sour cream	¾ teaspoon ground
	cinnamon

1. Heat the oven to 325°F. Grease and flour two 8½- by 4½-inch loaf pans. In a large bowl, with an electric mixer on high speed, beat the eggs, honey, sugar, oil, orange juice, sour cream, and orange rind until combined. In a medium-size bowl, combine the flour, baking powder, baking soda, and cinnamon. With the mixer on low speed, slowly beat the flour mixture into the egg mixture just until combined. Divide the batter between the prepared pans.

2. Bake the cakes 45 minutes. Reduce the oven temperature to 300°F and bake 15 to 25 minutes longer, or until a cake tester inserted in the center comes out clean. Cool the cakes in the pans on wire racks for 10 minutes. Invert the pans, unmold the cakes, and cool completely on the racks.

OVEN CHECKUP

Calibrate your oven temperature every so often. Even a trusted thermostat can cause a variance in temperatures of 10° to 15°F. Make allowances for this in setting your gauge and determining baking time.

Lime Tea Cake

Perhaps the British invented teatime just so the whole world could bake tea cakes. This one combines light citrus and crunchy pecan flavors. Don't skip the glaze. It adds a moist, sweet tang that provides a perfect finish to the cake.

MAKES 10 SERVINGS

½ cup (1 stick) butter or margarine, softened
¾ cup granulated sugar
2 eggs
2¼ cups cake flour
2 teaspoons baking powder
¼ teaspoon salt
⅓ cup milk

½ cup finely chopped pecans or walnuts
2 tablespoons lime juice
2 teaspoons grated lime rind

Lime Glaze:
¼ cup lime juice
⅓ cup confectioners' sugar

1. Heat the oven to 350°F. Lightly grease and flour a 9- by 5- by 3-inch loaf pan. In a large bowl, with an electric mixer on medium speed, beat the butter and granulated sugar until light and fluffy. Add the eggs, one at a time, beating well after each addition.

2. In a large sifter, combine the flour, baking powder, and salt. Sift the flour mixture over the butter mixture; add the milk. With the mixer on low speed, beat, scraping the bowl frequently, just until combined. Fold the pecans, lime juice, and lime rind into the batter. Pour the batter into the prepared pan.

3. Bake the cake 40 to 45 minutes, or until a cake tester inserted in the center comes out clean. Just before the cake has finished baking, prepare the Lime Glaze: In a small saucepan, combine the lime juice and confectioners' sugar. Cook over low heat, stirring constantly, until the sugar dissolves and the mixture is smooth.

4. As soon as the cake is removed from the oven, while it is still in the pan, pour the glaze over it. Cool the cake in the pan on a wire rack for 15 minutes. Remove the cake from the pan, and cool completely on the wire rack.

Stenciled Star Cake (above), page 84; and Doily Cake (below), page 30

Real Strawberry Shortcakes, page 56

Sugarless, Eggless Cake

By 1915, the country was at war and the American home baker had to learn to make cakes without the precious rationed foods. This one substitutes molasses for sugar and vegetable oil for butter. (During the war, chicken fat was the butter substitute!) If corn flour is unavailable, place ¾ cup cornmeal in a food processor fitted with the chopping blade and process until finely ground. The corn flour should measure 1 cup.

MAKES 8 SERVINGS

¾ cup molasses
¼ cup vegetable oil
1¼ cups all-purpose flour
1 cup corn flour
1 cup milk
4 teaspoons baking powder
2 teaspoons ground cinnamon
½ teaspoon salt
¼ teaspoon ground cloves
1 cup dark seedless raisins

Sugarless Glaze (optional):
¼ cup milk
2 tablespoons light corn syrup
1 teaspoon cornstarch
¼ teaspoon almond extract

1. Heat the oven to 350°F. Grease and flour an 8½- by 4½-inch loaf pan. In a large bowl, with an electric mixer on medium speed, beat the molasses and oil until fluffy. Reduce the mixer speed to low, and beat in the flour, corn flour, milk, baking powder, cinnamon, salt, and cloves just until smooth. Stir in the raisins. Spoon the batter into the prepared pan.

2. Bake the cake 60 to 65 minutes, or until a cake tester inserted in the center comes out clean. Cool the cake in the pan on a wire rack for 10 minutes. Remove the cake from the pan, and cool completely on the wire rack.

3. If desired, just before serving, prepare the Sugarless Glaze: In a 1-quart saucepan, combine the milk, corn syrup, and cornstarch until smooth; heat to boiling. Stir in the almond extract. Place the cake on a serving plate. Drizzle the glaze over the cake. If glazed, cover and refrigerate any remaining cake up to 2 days.

Chocolate Peanut Butter Cupcakes

....

A chocolate and peanut butter center is the rich surprise in these cupcakes. We use ordinary supermarket peanut butter — not the fancy gourmet kind. These taste best after they have cooled completely.

MAKES 1 DOZEN CUPCAKES

Chocolate Peanut Butter
Filling:
2 tablespoons heavy cream
2 1-ounce squares semisweet
chocolate, finely chopped
2 teaspoons granulated sugar
¼ cup peanut butter

6 1-ounce squares semisweet
chocolate

6 tablespoons (¾ stick)
butter or margarine
2 eggs
⅔ cup granulated sugar
1 teaspoon vanilla extract
¾ cup all-purpose flour
¼ teaspoon baking soda
¼ teaspoon salt
Confectioners' sugar
(optional)

1. An hour before baking, prepare the Chocolate Peanut Butter Filling: In a small saucepan, heat the cream to boiling. Add the chocolate and 2 teaspoons granulated sugar, stirring until the chocolate melts. Remove from the heat, and beat in the peanut butter until well combined. Refrigerate the mixture until firm but not hard, about 40 minutes.

2. Line twelve 2½-inch muffin-pan cups with paper baking cups. In the top of a double boiler, over simmering water, melt the chocolate and butter. Remove from the heat and set aside. In a large bowl, with an electric mixer on high speed, beat the eggs until foamy. Beat in the ⅔ cup granulated sugar and vanilla until the mixture is fluffy and lemon colored, about 5 minutes. Reduce the mixer speed to low, and slowly beat in the chocolate-butter mixture; beat in the flour, baking soda, and salt just until combined.

3. Heat the oven to 350°F. Divide the batter among the prepared muffin-pan cups. Using the palms of the hands, roll rounded teaspoonfuls of the chocolate-peanut butter filling into 12 balls. Push one ball into the center of the batter in each muffin-pan cup. (Make sure the chocolate peanut butter ball is covered by the cupcake batter.)

4. Bake the cupcakes 15 to 20 minutes, or until the center springs back when touched lightly with a fingertip. Cool the cupcakes completely in the pan on a wire rack. Remove the cupcakes from the pan. If desired, cover the centers of the cupcakes with small pieces of aluminum foil or paper towel, and sift confectioners' sugar over the edges. Remove the foil or towel. Store the cupcakes in an airtight container.

THE FROSTING ON THE CAKE

A beautifully frosted cake entices the eye before the palate. Many professional bakers swear by these techniques for their pretty cakes.

Place the cake to be frosted on a piece of cardboard cut to the same size as the cake. This allows you to frost it and then easily place it on any serving plate. Another reliable method calls for laying strips of waxed paper or aluminum foil on the edge of a serving plate and placing the cake layer on top. The strips will catch any frosting drippings. When you finish, remove the strips and the serving plate is clean.

For a layer cake, lightly brush crumbs from the side of the cake layer with your fingers. Gently place the first layer top side down on the serving plate or cardboard. Use a long metal spatula or a table knife to spread the top with frosting almost to the edge. Place the next layer top side up on the first layer and apply a small amount of frosting to the side of the cake. Spread it gently and evenly, adding small amounts until the entire side of the cake is frosted. Some bakers call this their first coat as it smooths out imperfections in the surface of the cake. Spoon some of the remaining frosting on top and apply a thin coat. Refrigerate 20 minutes to firm up the first coat and apply the second coat in the same way. Use a wet knife blade or the back of a spoon to swirl or smooth the frosting.

Chocolate-Frosted Cupcakes

These cupcakes are enormous fun for children to make, since kids "frost" them by simply letting a piece of their favorite chocolate bar melt on cupcakes hot from the oven. Sliced almonds, coconut, and candy sprinkles are the favored final touches.

MAKES 6 CUPCAKES

½ cup sugar
3 tablespoons butter or
   margarine, softened
1 egg
2 tablespoons milk
½ teaspoon vanilla extract
⅔ cup cake flour
½ teaspoon baking powder
⅛ teaspoon salt
2 1.45-ounce dark chocolate
   candy bars or 2¹⁵⁄₁₆-ounce
   white chocolate with
   almonds candy bars,
   or 1 of each

Toppings (optional):
¼ cup sliced almonds, or
   ¼ cup flaked coconut,
   or ¼ cup multi-colored
   candy sprinkles

1. Heat the oven to 350°F. Line six 2½-inch muffin-pan cups with paper baking cups. In a medium-size bowl, with an electric mixer on high speed, beat the sugar, butter, and egg until smooth and fluffy. Add the milk and vanilla; beat the mixture until smooth.

2. In a sifter, combine the flour, baking powder, and salt; sift over the butter mixture. With the mixer on low speed, beat the batter until smooth. Divide the batter among the prepared muffin-pan cups.

3. Bake the cupcakes 20 to 25 minutes, or until a cake tester inserted in the centers comes out clean. Meanwhile, cut each chocolate bar crosswise into 3 equal pieces. Remove the cupcakes from the oven and immediately top each one with a piece of chocolate. Let stand until the chocolate melts, about 2 minutes. With a knife, spread the chocolate to frost the tops of the cupcakes. Remove the cupcakes from the pan and cool completely on a wire rack. If desired, decorate the cupcakes with nuts, coconut, or sprinkles.

Currant Cakes

....

These are tender-sweet little muffin-like cupcakes with a hint of rose-water fragrance. They're perfect with breakfast, or serve them piled in a basket on a brunch buffet. Buy dried currants in good health-food stores and specialty food shops.

MAKES 2 DOZEN MINIATURE CUPCAKES

½ cup (1 stick) butter, softened
½ cup granulated sugar
2 eggs
2 tablespoons milk
2 tablespoons Drambuie or orange juice

1 teaspoon rose water or vanilla extract
¾ cup all-purpose flour
1 teaspoon baking powder
¼ teaspoon salt
¼ cup dried currants
Confectioners' sugar (optional)

1. Heat the oven to 350°F. Grease twenty-four 1¾-inch miniature muffin-pan cups. In a medium-size bowl, with an electric mixer on medium speed, beat the butter and granulated sugar until light and fluffy. Beat in the eggs, milk, Drambuie, and rose water until well combined.

2. Reduce the mixer speed to low, and beat in the flour, baking powder, and salt, scraping the side of the bowl occasionally, until well combined. Stir in the currants. Divide the batter among the prepared muffin-pan cups.

3. Bake the cakes 10 to 15 minutes, or until a cake tester inserted in the centers comes out clean. Cool the cupcakes in the pan on a wire rack for 5 minutes. Remove the cupcakes from the pan, and cool completely on the rack. If desired, sprinkle with confectioners' sugar before serving.

Spice Cupcakes with Cocoa Frosting

....

These are our favorites! They are truly moist and full of spice. The rich buttercream frosting makes them irresistible. If they last more than a day, be sure to store them in an airtight container.

MAKES 18 CUPCAKES

½ cup (1 stick) butter or
  margarine, softened
2 cups cake flour
¾ cup firmly packed
  light-brown sugar
2 teaspoons baking powder
½ teaspoon salt
⅔ cup water
3 eggs
1 teaspoon ground cinnamon
½ teaspoon ground nutmeg
¼ teaspoon ground allspice
¼ teaspoon ground cloves

Cocoa Buttercream Frosting:
½ cup (1 stick) butter or
  margarine, softened
½ cup cocoa powder
⅓ cup milk
1 teaspoon vanilla extract
2¾ to 3 cups confectioners'
  sugar
1 1-ounce square semisweet
  chocolate, grated
  (optional)

1. Heat the oven to 375°F. Line eighteen 2½-inch muffin-pan cups with paper baking cups. In a large bowl, with an electric mixer on medium speed, beat the butter until fluffy. Reduce the mixer speed to low and beat in the flour, brown sugar, baking powder, salt, water, eggs, and spices, scraping the bowl frequently, just until the mixture is moistened. Increase the mixer speed to medium, and beat the mixture until smooth and fluffy, about 1 minute. Divide the batter among the prepared muffin-pan cups.

2. Bake the cupcakes 15 to 20 minutes, or until a cake tester inserted in the centers comes out clean. Cool the cupcakes completely in the pans on wire racks. Remove the cupcakes from the pans.

3. Prepare the Cocoa Buttercream Frosting: In a small bowl, with the mixer on low speed, beat the butter, cocoa, milk, and vanilla, scraping the bowl frequently, until well mixed. Gradually beat in the confectioners' sugar until the frosting is stiff enough to spread. Spread the frosting over the top of each cupcake. If desired, sprinkle the cupcakes with the grated chocolate.

Date Cake

....

This is a simple one-pan snack cake topped with chopped sweet dates and nuts. Chopping dried dates for this recipe can be messy. Sometimes it is helpful to run the knife under hot water before cutting the dates. Or try lightly dusting the dates with flour before chopping to prevent sticking.

MAKES 9 SERVINGS

1 cup boiling water
1 cup finely chopped pitted dates
1 teaspoon baking soda
1 egg, beaten
1 cup sugar
1 tablespoon butter or margarine, melted
1½ cups all-purpose flour

1½ teaspoons baking powder
1 teaspoon vanilla extract

Date-Nut Topping:
1 cup sugar
½ cup chopped pitted dates
½ cup water
½ cup chopped walnuts, almonds, or pistachios

1. Heat the oven to 325°F. Grease and flour a 9-inch square baking pan. In a large bowl, pour the boiling water over the dates and baking soda. In a small bowl, combine the egg, sugar, and butter until well mixed. Stir in the date mixture.

2. Into a small bowl, sift the flour and baking powder. Add the flour mixture to the date mixture; stir in the vanilla. Pour the batter into the prepared pan.

3. Bake the cake 45 to 55 minutes, or until a cake tester inserted in the center comes out clean. Cool the cake completely in the pan on a wire rack.

4. Prepare the Date-Nut Topping: In a 1-quart saucepan, cook the sugar, dates, and water over medium heat until thick and bubbly. Remove the saucepan from the heat. Stir in the walnuts. Spread the topping over the cooled cake. To serve, cut the cake into squares.

Zucchini Fudge Cake
PHOTOGRAPH ON PAGE 54

An unusual buttermilk-chocolate-zucchini combination, this moist cake is four layers high, studded with walnuts and topped with a dense fudge frosting. We suggest serving it with whipped cream and fresh raspberries.

MAKES 12 SERVINGS

4 eggs
2¼ cups granulated sugar
2 teaspoons vanilla extract
¾ cup (1 ½ sticks) butter or
   margarine, softened
3 cups all-purpose flour
½ cup cocoa powder
2 teaspoons baking powder
1 teaspoon baking soda
¾ teaspoon salt
1 cup buttermilk
3 cups coarsely shredded
   zucchini
1 cup chopped walnuts

Chocolate Frosting:
1 cup (2 sticks) butter or
   margarine, softened
2 1-pound packages
   confectioners' sugar
½ cup cocoa powder
1 tablespoon vanilla extract
⅓ to ½ cup milk

½ 4-ounce bar dark
   chocolate
½ cup whipped cream
   (optional)
1 half-pint basket (1 cup)
   raspberries (optional)

1. Grease and flour four 9-inch round baking pans. Heat the oven to 350°F. In a large bowl, with an electric mixer on high speed, beat the eggs until light and fluffy. Gradually add the granulated sugar, beating until the mixture is very thick and lemon colored, about 5 minutes. Gradually beat in the vanilla and butter.

2. In a large sifter, combine the flour, cocoa, baking powder, baking soda, and salt. Sift half the flour mixture over the egg mixture. With the mixer on low speed, beat until well mixed. Beat in the buttermilk until combined. Sift in the remaining flour mixture and beat until combined. Fold in the zucchini and walnuts. Divide the batter among the prepared pans.

3. Bake the cakes 25 to 30 minutes, or until a cake tester inserted in the center comes out clean. Cool the cakes in the pans on wire racks

10 minutes. Remove the cakes from the pans and cool completely on the racks.

4. Prepare the Chocolate Frosting: In a large bowl, with the mixer on medium speed, beat the butter, confectioners' sugar, cocoa, vanilla, and milk until creamy. Spoon 1 cup of the frosting into a pastry bag fitted with a small star tip; set aside. Place one cake layer on a serving plate; spread the top with ⅓ cup frosting. Place a second cake layer on top of the first, and spread the top with ⅓ cup frosting. Place a third cake layer on top of the second, and spread the top with ⅓ cup frosting. Top with the remaining cake layer. Spread the top and side of the cake with the remaining frosting. With the pastry bag, pipe a shell border around the top and bottom of the cake. With a vegetable peeler, shave the chocolate over the cake. If desired, serve the cake with whipped cream and raspberries.

FROM CAKE TO CUPCAKE

Most cake recipes will convert easily to make cupcakes. Use 2½-inch muffin-pan cups and fill each cup up to two thirds full with your favorite batter. Reduce the cake baking time to 15 or 20 minutes. Don't try converting dense fruitcakes or even foam cakes. The results are usually dry and disappointing.

One 8-inch square cake = 12 cupcakes
One 9- by 13-inch cake = 18 cupcakes
Two 9-inch round layers = 24 cupcakes
Two 8-inch round layers = 18 cupcakes

Caramel-Apple Spice Cake

For the apple lover! This is a rustic frontier layer cake with a wheaty-walnut flavor and a classic box-social look. A thick filling of tart apples and cherries is spread between the layers and golden caramelized apple slices are piled on top.

1½ cups firmly packed light-brown sugar
1 cup vegetable oil
3 eggs
½ cup apple juice
1 teaspoon vanilla extract
2 cups all-purpose flour
½ cup whole-wheat flour
2 teaspoons baking powder
2 teaspoons ground cinnamon
1 teaspoon ground ginger
½ teaspoon ground cloves
½ teaspoon salt
1 cup chopped walnuts

Apple-Cherry Filling:
2 medium-size Granny Smith apples, peeled, cored, and finely chopped
½ cup dried tart cherries
½ cup apple juice
¼ teaspoon ground cinnamon

Caramel-Apple Topping:
½ cup granulated sugar
½ cup water
3 medium-size Granny Smith apples
2 tablespoons heavy cream

Vanilla ice cream or frozen yogurt (optional)

1. Heat the oven to 350°F. Line the bottom of two 9-inch round baking pans with waxed paper. Grease and flour the lined pans. In a large bowl, with an electric mixer on medium speed, beat the brown sugar and oil until well blended; add the eggs, apple juice, and vanilla and beat until smooth.

2. In a medium-size bowl, combine both flours, the baking powder, cinnamon, ginger, cloves, and salt. With the mixer on low speed, beat the flour mixture into the brown sugar mixture until a smooth batter forms. Stir the walnuts into the batter and divide evenly between the prepared pans.

3. Bake the cakes 35 to 40 minutes, or until a cake tester inserted in the center comes out clean. Cool the cakes in the pans on wire racks for 5 minutes, remove the pans, and cool completely on the racks.

4. Meanwhile, prepare the Apple-Cherry Filling: In a 2-quart saucepan, combine the chopped apples, dried cherries, juice, and cinnamon. Cover and cook over medium-low heat until the apples and cherries are soft, about 15 minutes. Remove half the apple-cherry mixture to a blender or food processor fitted with the chopping blade; process until smooth. Return the mixture to the saucepan; blend with the remaining apple-cherry mixture.

5. Prepare the Caramel-Apple Topping: In a large skillet, combine the granulated sugar and water; heat over low heat, stirring gently, until the sugar is dissolved. Increase the heat to medium and cook, without stirring, until the mixture is a dark, golden brown, about 5 minutes. Meanwhile, peel, core, and slice the apples; set aside. When the sugar mixture is dark, golden brown, remove from the heat and carefully stir in the cream to the make the caramel. The mixture will bubble up but recede as it cools. Add the apple slices to the caramel. Cook over low heat 5 minutes. Remove from the heat; set aside to cool completely.

6. To assemble the cake, place one cake layer on a serving plate. Spread the top with the apple-cherry filling; place the other cake layer on top of the first. With a slotted spoon, arrange the cooled apple slices on the top of the cake; drizzle the remaining caramel syrup over the cake. If desired, serve with vanilla ice cream.

M I C R O W A V E   C H O C O L A T E   P I P I N G

For a quick decorative transformation of a plain frosted cake, place a 1-ounce square of semisweet chocolate in a small zip-close heavyweight plastic bag and microwave on medium 1 minute. Knead the bag gently, then microwave on medium 1 minute more, until the chocolate is melted. Snip off a little of one corner and drizzle the chocolate in a spiral or any other decorative pattern over the top of the cake.

Sour Cream Gingerbread

The least gingery of all gingerbreads, this one does not have a spicy tang but instead a very mild flavor and an airy, moist, cake-like texture. We like it best served warm, with a dollop of whipped cream or vanilla ice cream.

MAKES 9 SERVINGS

2 eggs
½ cup light molasses
½ cup sour cream
*½ cup firmly packed
   light-brown sugar*
1½ cups cake flour
1 teaspoon baking soda

1 teaspoon ground ginger
¼ teaspoon salt
*½ cup (1 stick) butter or
   margarine, melted*
*1 cup whipped cream
   (optional)*

1. Heat the oven to 350°F. Grease an 8-inch square baking pan. In a large bowl, with an electric mixer on medium speed, beat the eggs until foamy. Beat in the molasses, sour cream, and sugar until smooth.

2. Into a small bowl, sift the flour, baking soda, ginger, and salt. With the mixer on low speed, beat the flour mixture into the egg mixture until smooth; stir in the butter. Pour the batter into the prepared pan.

3. Bake the gingerbread 25 minutes, or until a cake tester inserted in the center comes out clean. Cool the gingerbread in the pan on a wire rack for 10 minutes. Serve the gingerbread warm or cool, cut into squares. If desired, top with whipped cream.

QUICK TIP

If the recipe requires that you soak dried fruit in water or juice to plump it up before baking, here's a time saver. Place ½ cup dried fruit with 2 tablespoons orange juice or water in a 1-quart microwave-safe bowl. Cover lightly with waxed paper and microwave on high 2 minutes. Let stand about 5 minutes.

One-Two-Three-Four Cake

············

Named so that the quantities of the main ingredients could be easily remembered, this cake is from the days when recipes were passed on verbally. Fill and frost with Chocolate Frosting as on page 44, Apple-Cherry Filling as on page 46, simple whipped cream, or your own favorite finish.

MAKES 12 SERVINGS

1 cup (2 sticks) butter, softened	2½ teaspoons baking powder
2 cups sugar	1 cup milk
4 eggs	2 teaspoons vanilla extract
3 cups sifted cake flour	

1. Heat the oven to 350°F. Grease and flour two 9-inch round baking pans. In a large bowl, with an electric mixer on medium speed, beat the butter and sugar until light and fluffy. Add the eggs, one at a time, beating well after each addition.

2. In a medium-size bowl, combine the flour and baking powder. With the mixer on low speed, and beginning and ending with the flour mixture, alternately beat the flour mixture and the milk and vanilla into the butter mixture until just combined. Do not overbeat. Divide the batter between the prepared pans.

3. Bake the cakes 30 to 35 minutes, or until a cake tester inserted in the center comes out clean. Cool the cakes in the pans on wire racks for 5 minutes. Remove the cakes from the pans and cool completely on the wire racks.

SHOWING OFF

If you have a choice, select a serving plate that best shows off your cake. Rustic, delicate, romantic, whimsical, antique, and playful plates may all be suitable for different cakes and/or occasions. A pedestal cake stand is a wonderful way to display a cake, too, and a dome is a storing help.

Cranberry Upside-Down Cake

It didn't take the Colonists long to find an upside-down use for the Massachusetts cranberry. This cake bakes in a springform pan rather than a skillet and when unmolded it has an uptown character suitable for any holiday table.

MAKES 8 SERVINGS

4 cups fresh or frozen
    unthawed cranberries
2¼ cups sugar
¾ cup (1½ sticks) butter or
    margarine, softened
¼ cup red currant jelly
¼ cup orange juice
2 tablespoons cornstarch
1 teaspoon grated, peeled
    fresh gingerroot
1 teaspoon grated orange
    rind

2 cups cake flour
½ teaspoon baking powder
½ teaspoon baking soda
½ teaspoon salt
3 eggs
1 teaspoon almond extract
1 cup buttermilk
Sprigs fresh mint for garnish
    (optional)
Fresh cranberries (optional)

1. Grease a 9-inch springform pan; line the bottom with waxed paper and grease the paper. In a 2-quart saucepan, combine 1 cup cranberries, 1 cup sugar, ¼ cup butter, the red currant jelly, orange juice, cornstarch, gingerroot, and orange rind. Cook over medium heat, stirring constantly, until the mixture boils and thickens, about 10 minutes.

2. Remove the saucepan from the heat; drain off and reserve ⅓ cup syrup from the mixture and set aside. Stir the remaining 3 cups cranberries and ¼ cup of the remaining sugar into the mixture in the saucepan. Set aside to cool.

3. Heat the oven to 325°F. Into a medium-size bowl, sift the flour, baking powder, baking soda, and salt; set aside. In a large bowl, with an electric mixer on medium speed, beat the remaining 1 cup sugar and ½ cup butter until light and fluffy. Add the eggs, one at a time, beating well after each addition. Beat in the almond extract.

4. Reduce the mixer speed to low, and beginning and ending with the flour mixture, alternately beat the flour mixture and the buttermilk

into the butter mixture until well combined. Spread the cooled cranberry mixture in an even layer in the bottom of the prepared pan; spoon the batter evenly over the cranberry mixture. Place the pan on a rimmed baking sheet.

5. Bake the cake 60 to 65 minutes, or until a cake tester inserted in the center comes out clean. Cool the cake in the pan on a wire rack for 45 minutes. Invert the pan, and unmold the cake onto a serving plate; remove the waxed paper. Drizzle the reserved ⅓ cup syrup on the cake and cut into 8 wedges. Place each wedge on an individual serving plate, and, if desired, garnish with mint and cranberries.

H O M E M A D E   P R I O R I T Y   M A I L

Dense pound cakes, tea cakes, fruitcakes, and buttery Bundt cakes are easy to pack and will arrive safe and fresh to even far-away destinations through the mails. They make great I-miss-you gifts, holiday presents, and happy birthday surprise packages.

Wrap the cake in plastic wrap or aluminum foil and place it in a sturdy box that is slightly larger than the cake. Pack the box and the area surrounding the cake with dependable cushioning material — plastic styrofoam bubbles, bubble wrap, tissue paper, and crumpled newspaper are all good choices. Seal the box and mail. If the cake is being mailed within the USA, we suggest overnight or 2nd-day mail. However, the cake will remain fresh and flavorful for several days and can travel through the slower mails.

Delicate cakes such as chiffon and angel food must be wrapped tightly in plastic wrap or aluminum foil and sent through the mail only if you can be sure they will arrive within two days. To pack these cakes, place them on top of packing materials in a very sturdy box. Surround the cake top, sides, and bottom with the packing material so that the cake is totally suspended and supported by the packing material on all sides. Seal the box and send it off.

Carrot Cake

....

It wasn't until the 70s that carrot cake coated with a sweet cream cheese frosting became a fad — the perfect way for the newly health conscious to have their cake and veggies too.

MAKES 12 SERVINGS

4 eggs
1½ cups granulated sugar
¾ cup vegetable oil
¼ cup orange juice
1 teaspoon vanilla extract
2 cups all-purpose flour
2 teaspoons ground cinnamon
1½ teaspoons baking soda
1 teaspoon baking powder
½ teaspoon salt
2 cups coarsely shredded
   carrots

Cream Cheese Frosting:
1 8-ounce package cream
   cheese, softened
1 1-pound package
   confectioners' sugar
1 teaspoon vanilla extract
1 to 2 teaspoons milk

½ cup pecan halves for
   garnish

1. Heat the oven to 350°F. Grease and flour two 9-inch round baking pans. In a large bowl, with an electric mixer on medium speed, beat the eggs, granulated sugar, oil, orange juice, and vanilla until combined. Reduce the mixer speed to low and beat in the flour, cinnamon, baking soda, baking powder, and salt until the batter is smooth. Gently fold in the carrots. Divide the batter evenly between the prepared pans.

2. Bake the cakes 30 minutes, or until a cake tester inserted in the center comes out clean. Cool the cakes in the pans on wire racks for 5 minutes. Remove the cakes from the pans, and cool completely on the racks.

3. Prepare the Cream Cheese Frosting: In a medium-size bowl, with the mixer on medium speed, beat the cream cheese, confectioners' sugar, vanilla, and milk until smooth.

4. To assemble the cake, place one cake layer on a serving plate. Spread the top with ⅓ cup of the cream cheese frosting. Place the other cake layer on top of the first. Spread the top and side of the cake with the remaining frosting. Arrange the pecans in a circle along the top border of the cake. Refrigerate until ready to serve.

Black-and-White Cake, page 62

Zucchini Fudge Cake, page 44

Wild-Blueberry Cake

....

We think wild blueberries are one of America's finest natural resources. They thrive throughout the Northeast, even in New York City's Central Park. Buy dried berries in good health-food shops and specialty food stores. They're sold just like raisins, in 4-, 6-, and 8-ounce packages.

MAKES 10 SERVINGS

¾ cup dried wild
   blueberries
3 tablespoons dry sherry or
   brandy
2 cups all-purpose flour
½ cup yellow cornmeal
1 teaspoon baking powder
½ teaspoon baking soda
½ teaspoon salt

1 cup (2 sticks) butter or
   margarine, softened
1½ cups plus 1 tablespoon
   confectioners' sugar
2 eggs
1 cup buttermilk
½ cup finely ground pecans
2 teaspoons grated orange
   rind

1. In a small bowl, combine the dried blueberries and sherry; let the mixture stand 1 hour. Drain the blueberries, reserving any liquid, and set aside.

2. Heat the oven to 350°F. Generously grease and flour a 10-inch Bundt or tube pan. In a medium-size bowl, combine the flour, cornmeal, baking powder, baking soda, and salt.

3. In a large bowl, with an electric mixer on medium speed, beat the butter and 1½ cups confectioners' sugar until light and fluffy. Add the eggs, one at a time, beating well after each addition. Reduce the mixer speed to low, and beginning and ending with the flour mixture, alternately beat the flour mixture and the buttermilk and the liquid reserved from the blueberries into the butter mixture, until just combined. Fold the blueberries, pecans, and orange rind into the batter. Spoon the batter into the prepared pan.

4. Bake the cake 40 to 45 minutes, or until a cake tester inserted in the center comes out clean. Cool the cake in the pan on a wire rack for 10 minutes. Remove the cake from the pan, and cool completely on the rack. Place the cake on a serving plate. Sift the remaining 1 tablespoon confectioners' sugar over the cake before serving.

Real Strawberry Shortcakes

PHOTOGRAPH ON PAGE 36

A tender and buttery shortcake biscuit, split in half, layered with straw-berries and topped with whipped cream is a traditional summertime dessert, with a brief baking period that keeps the kitchen cool. The secret here is to bake the biscuits at the last minute and serve them warm.

MAKES 6 SERVINGS

4 cups all-purpose flour
4 teaspoons baking powder
6 tablespoons sugar
1 teaspoon salt
¼ teaspoon ground nutmeg
¾ cup (1½ sticks) butter
1½ cups milk

Strawberry Filling:
2 pint baskets (4 cups) ripe
    strawberries

2 tablespoons granulated
    sugar

Whipped Cream:
2 cups (1 pint) heavy cream
2 tablespoons confectioners'
    sugar
1 teaspoon vanilla extract

1. Heat the oven to 425°F. Grease a baking sheet. In a large bowl, combine the flour, baking powder, 5 tablespoons sugar, salt, and nut-meg. With a pastry blender or 2 knives, cut ½ cup of the butter into the flour mixture until the mixture resembles coarse crumbs. In a small saucepan, melt the remaining ¼ cup butter over medium heat; set aside.

2. Stir the milk into the flour mixture until a soft dough forms. Knead the dough in the bowl until smooth, 1 to 2 minutes. Turn onto lightly floured surface, and roll out to a 1-inch thickness. With cookie cutters or round glasses, cut out six 2½-inch rounds and six 3-inch rounds.

3. Place the 3-inch rounds on the prepared baking sheet. Brush each with some of the melted butter and top with a 2½-inch round. Brush the tops with butter. Sprinkle with the remaining 1 tablespoon sugar.

4. Bake the biscuits 12 to 14 minutes, or until golden brown. Cool the biscuits slightly on wire racks.

5. Meanwhile, prepare the Strawberry Filling: Rinse and hull the strawberries; pat dry with paper towels. Set aside half the strawberries, selecting the most attractive ones for the tops of the shortcakes. Into a medium-size bowl, slice the remaining strawberries and sprinkle with 2 tablespoons granulated sugar. Let stand at room temperature 30 minutes.

6. Prepare the Whipped Cream: In a medium-size bowl, with an electric mixer on medium speed, beat the cream, confectioners' sugar, and vanilla until stiff peaks form.

7. Split the shortcakes in half. Place each bottom half on a serving plate. Divide the strawberry filling among the bottom halves. Place the biscuit tops on the strawberries. Spoon some of the whipped cream on each top. Garnish each shortcake with one of the reserved strawberries and serve with any remaining strawberries and whipped cream.

KEEPING THE CAKE: LEFTOVERS

Most fresh cakes will lose their flavor after a couple of days. So if you have no plans for leftovers, sending cake home with your dinner guests sometimes gets the best life from the cake and certainly nurtures friendships.

For next-day lunch, dinner, or snacks, store cake without frostings or icings either covered with plastic wrap or stored in an airtight cake keeper at room temperature.

Cakes frosted or filled with whipped cream must be kept in the refrigerator. Cakes frosted with buttercream or confectioners' sugar will keep one day in a cool place in the kitchen or pantry, covered loosely with plastic wrap or placed in a cake keeper. To keep these cakes 2 to 3 days, store in the refrigerator, covered loosely with plastic wrap. Tuck the plastic wrap under the serving plate or plastic round to keep the cake from absorbing odors.

Pumpkin Shortcakes with Fall Fruit Filling

Not at all your ordinary shortcakes, these individual desserts fairly burst with the rich and spicy aromatic fruits of autumn. Orange, ginger, cranberry, apple, prune, clove, cinnamon, and walnut come together served atop creamy pumpkin shortcakes. This is a good dish to make on Thanksgiving Sunday, to use up small quantities of fruits and nuts left over from the holiday feast. With this recipe, the filling and cakes can be made several hours ahead and the dessert assembled at the last minute.

MAKES 12 SERVINGS

2½ cups all-purpose flour
⅓ cup granulated sugar
1 tablespoon baking powder
½ teaspoon ground nutmeg
½ teaspoon salt
6 tablespoons butter
1 cup canned pumpkin or
   fresh pumpkin puree
⅔ cup heavy cream
2 teaspoons grated, peeled,
   fresh gingerroot

Fall Fruit Filling:
2 tablespoons butter
¼ cup firmly packed
   dark-brown sugar
½ teaspoon ground
   cinnamon

½ teaspoon grated, peeled,
   fresh gingerroot
½ teaspoon grated orange
   rind
⅛ teaspoon ground cloves
½ cup apple juice
¼ cup chopped pitted prunes
1 Granny Smith apple, cored
   and finely chopped
¼ cup fresh cranberries
⅓ cup chopped toasted
   walnuts

Whipped Cream:
⅔ cup heavy cream
1 tablespoon confectioners'
   sugar

1. Heat the oven to 375°F. In a large bowl, combine the flour, granulated sugar, baking powder, nutmeg, and salt. With a pastry blender or 2 knives, cut the butter into the flour mixture until the mixture resembles coarse crumbs.

2. In a small bowl, combine the pumpkin, cream, and 2 teaspoons gingerroot. Stir the pumpkin mixture into the flour mixture just until combined; do not overmix.

3. Grease 2 baking sheets. Drop the shortcake dough, ¼ cupful at a time, onto the baking sheets. Pinch the tops of the shortcakes to create small mounds. Bake the shortcakes 25 minutes, or until they are slightly brown and the centers spring back when lightly pressed with a fingertip.

4. Meanwhile, prepare the Fall Fruit Filling: In a large skillet, melt the butter. Add the brown sugar, cinnamon, ½ teaspoon gingerroot, orange rind, and cloves. Cook over medium heat, stirring constantly, until the mixture is well blended and bubbly. Add the apple juice and prunes, and cook 2 minutes. Add the apple and cook, stirring occasionally, 5 minutes. Stir in the cranberries and cook until the cranberries soften but do not burst and the mixture becomes syrupy. Remove the filling from the heat and stir in the walnuts. Set aside to cool.

5. Prepare the Whipped Cream: Just before serving, in a small bowl, with an electric mixer on medium speed, beat the cream and confectioners' sugar until stiff peaks form.

6. To assemble the shortcakes, cut off the tops of the shortcakes and set aside. On individual serving plates, place a shortcake bottom and a generous tablespoon each of the fall fruit filling and the whipped cream. Replace the tops and serve immediately.

VEGETABLE CAKES

Adding fruits and vegetables to cake batter is not a newfangled notion. Country bakers have been doing it for as long as anyone can remember, and their German and Scandinavian ancestors were doing it long before immigrating to America. Carrots, squash, zucchini, apples, bananas, pumpkin, and prunes all add moisture.

Pumpkin and sweet potatoes are usually cooked and mashed before being incorporated into the batter. Zucchini and carrots bring more moisture and flavor to the cake if they are grated and added raw. A medium to large coarse shred is best, so grate them using the large holes of a hand grater or the shredding disk of a food processor. Don't be tempted to squeeze any moisture from the freshly grated zucchini, as that is one of its big gifts to your cake.

Red-Raspberry Torte

In classic style, this torte is four layers of light cake filled with butter-cream and sweet berry jam. You can bake the cakes in batches if you have only two pans.

MAKES 16 SERVINGS

Berry Filling:
1 10-ounce package frozen
*   red raspberries, thawed*
2 tablespoons cornstarch

2⅓ cups granulated sugar
1⅓ cups butter, softened
8 eggs, separated, at room
*   temperature*
2½ cups all-purpose flour
1 teaspoon baking powder

Buttercream Frosting:
½ cup (1 stick) butter,
*   softened*
1¾ cups confectioners' sugar
2 tablespoons milk
1 to 2 tablespoons
*   almond-flavored liqueur*
3 half-pint baskets (3 cups)
*   red raspberries, rinsed and*
*   well drained*

1. Prepare the Berry Filling: In a 1-quart saucepan, combine the thawed raspberries, their syrup, and the cornstarch. Cook over low heat, stirring constantly, until thickened and boiling. Boil 1 minute, then strain the filling into a medium-size bowl. Refrigerate the filling until ready to assemble the torte.

2. Heat the oven to 350°F. Grease four 9-inch round baking pans and line the bottoms with waxed paper; grease the paper. In a medium-size bowl, with an electric mixer on medium speed, beat 2 cups granulated sugar and the butter until light and fluffy. Add the egg yolks, one at a time, beating well after each addition and scraping the bowl occasionally, until well combined. Reduce the mixer speed to low, and beat the flour and baking powder into the egg yolk mixture until well blended.

3. In a large bowl, with clean beaters and the mixer on high speed, beat the egg whites until foamy. Gradually add the remaining ⅓ cup granulated sugar and beat until stiff peaks form. Fold the egg yolk mixture into the egg whites. Divide the batter among the prepared pans.

4. Bake the cakes 25 to 30 minutes, or until a cake tester inserted in the center comes out clean. Cool the cakes in the pans on wire racks for 5 minutes. Remove the cakes from the pans, and cool completely on the racks.

5. Meanwhile, prepare the Buttercream Frosting: In a medium-size bowl, with the mixer on medium speed, beat the butter, confectioners' sugar, milk, and 1 tablespoon liqueur until smooth and fluffy. If the mixture becomes too stiff to spread, add more liqueur.

6. To assemble the torte, place one cake layer on a serving plate. Spoon the frosting into a pastry bag fitted with a medium star tip. Pipe a double border around the top edge of the cake layer. Remove the berry filling from the refrigerator, and set aside 2 tablespoons. Fold 2 cups raspberries into the remaining filling. Spoon one third of the filling on top of the cake layer. Place a second cake layer on top of the first, pipe a double border around the top edge and spoon one third of the filling on the top. Repeat the process with the third cake layer. Top with the remaining cake layer. Combine the reserved 2 tablespoons filling and the remaining 1 cup raspberries, and spread on the top. Serve the torte immediately, or refrigerate until ready to serve.

ALWAYS IN GOOD TASTE

Good baking chocolate is delicate. Keep it in an airtight container or a heavy-duty plastic bag to preserve flavor and prevent it from absorbing odors. Store it in a cool place — it needn't be as cold as the refrigerator but shouldn't be warmer than 75°F.

Store extra unused egg whites in a jar with a tight-fitting lid in the refrigerator up to 4 days. Egg whites can also be frozen in a plastic container with a tight-fitting lid or frozen, one egg white to an individual ice cube mold. Once frozen, unmold the individual cubes and wrap them well in plastic. Thaw to room temperature before using.

Black-and-White Cake

PHOTOGRAPH ON PAGE 53

Here is an exciting contrast in tastes and textures — a dense and moist chocolate cream cheese cake layered between two light white chiffon layers and filled with rich cocoa cream. Make the black cake a day ahead as its flavor and texture benefit from the long chill.

MAKES 12 SERVINGS

Black Cake:
2 8-ounce packages cream
  cheese, softened
¾ cup granulated sugar
2 eggs
2 teaspoons vanilla extract
3 1-ounce squares semisweet
  chocolate, melted and
  cooled
1 cup sour cream

White Cake:
2 cups cake flour
1 tablespoon baking powder
½ teaspoon salt
1 cup granulated sugar
⅓ cup vegetable oil

3 eggs, separated, at room
  temperature
⅔ cup water
1 tablespoon vanilla extract
½ teaspoon cream of tartar

Chocolate-Dipped Walnuts:
1 1-ounce square semisweet
  chocolate, coarsely
  chopped
16 walnut halves

Cocoa Whipped Cream:
2 cups (1 pint) heavy cream
¼ cup confectioners' sugar
2 tablespoons cocoa powder
1 teaspoon vanilla extract

1. Heat the oven to 325°F. Grease a 9-inch springform pan and two 9-inch round baking pans. Line the bottoms of the pans with aluminum foil; grease the foil.

2. Prepare the Black Cake: In a large bowl, with an electric mixer on medium speed, beat the cream cheese until smooth and fluffy. Gradually beat in the ¾ cup granulated sugar. Add the eggs, one at a time, beating well after each addition. Fold in the vanilla, chocolate, and sour cream until blended.

3. Pour the cream cheese mixture into the prepared springform pan. Bake the cake 35 to 40 minutes, or until the center of the cake seems to

be almost set when the pan is gently shaken. Cool the cake completely in the pan on a wire rack. Remove the side of the pan and refrigerate the cake at least 4 hours.

4. Prepare the White Cake: In a large bowl, combine the flour, baking powder, salt, and ¾ cup granulated sugar. Make a well in the center of the flour mixture. Add the oil, egg yolks, water, and vanilla. With a wire whisk, beat the mixture until smooth.

5. In a small bowl, with an electric mixer on high speed, beat the egg whites and cream of tartar until frothy. Gradually beat in the remaining ¼ cup granulated sugar until stiff peaks form. Carefully fold the egg white mixture into the flour mixture until just combined.

6. Divide the batter between the prepared round baking pans. Bake the cakes 35 minutes, or until the centers spring back when lightly pressed with a fingertip. Cool the cakes in the pans on wire racks 10 minutes. Remove the cakes from the pans, and cool completely on the racks.

7. Prepare the Chocolate-Dipped Walnuts: In a small measuring cup, place the chocolate. Set the cup in a saucepan with hot, not boiling, water; let stand until the chocolate melts. Cover a small tray with waxed paper. Dip half of each walnut into the chocolate and place on the prepared tray. Refrigerate the walnuts until the chocolate sets.

8. To assemble the cake, prepare the Cocoa Whipped Cream: In a large bowl, with an electric mixer on medium speed, beat the cream, confectioners' sugar, cocoa, and vanilla until stiff peaks form.

9. Place one white cake layer, right side up, on a serving plate. Spread the top with ⅓ cup cocoa whipped cream. Invert the black cake layer on top of the white cake layer. Remove the bottom of the pan. Spread the black layer with ⅓ cup cocoa whipped cream. Top with remaining cake layer, right side up.

10. Spoon 1 cup cocoa whipped cream into a pastry bag fitted with a medium star tip and 1 cup into a pastry bag fitted with a large star tip. Spread top and side of cake with remaining cocoa whipped cream.

11. Using the pastry bag with the medium star tip, pipe the cream in diagonal stripes across the top of the cake. Repeat in the other direction to make a lattice. Using the pastry bag with the large star tip, pipe a border around the top and bottom edges of the cake. Decorate the cake with the chocolate-dipped walnuts. Refrigerate until ready to serve.

Cocoa Chiffon Cream Cake

This cake takes some doing and requires an overnight chilling after it is baked and assembled, but the creamy rich cocoa filling topped with raspberry preserves makes it well worth the time and effort.

MAKES 16 SERVINGS

8 eggs, at room temperature
¾ cup water
¼ cup vegetable oil
1⅔ cups cake flour
1 cup granulated sugar
½ cup cocoa powder
1½ teaspoons baking soda
½ teaspoon salt
1 teaspoon vanilla extract
½ teaspoon cream of tartar

Cocoa Filling:
1 cup (½ pint) heavy cream
2 tablespoons confectioners'
  sugar
2 tablespoons cocoa powder
½ teaspoon vanilla extract

¼ cup seedless raspberry
  preserves

1. Separate the eggs, placing all the whites in a large bowl and 4 yolks in a medium-size bowl. Cover and refrigerate or freeze the remaining yolks for use in another recipe.

2. Heat the oven to 325°F. With a wire whisk, beat the water and oil into the yolks until well combined. Stir the flour, ½ cup granulated sugar, cocoa, baking soda, and salt into the yolk mixture until smooth; stir in the vanilla. Set the batter aside.

3. With an electric mixer on high speed, beat the egg whites and cream of tartar until foamy. Gradually add the remaining ½ cup granulated sugar and continue to beat until stiff peaks form. Pour the batter over the egg whites, and gently fold together until just combined. Pour into an ungreased 10-inch tube pan.

4. Bake the cake 55 to 60 minutes, or until a cake tester inserted in the center comes out clean. Invert the pan over a bottle. Cool the cake completely in the pan, about 1 hour.

5. Meanwhile, prepare the Cocoa Filling: In a small bowl, combine the cream, confectioners' sugar, cocoa, and vanilla. Cover and refrigerate the cocoa filling 1 hour.

6. With a knife, loosen the edge of the cake, invert the pan, and unmold the cake onto a serving plate. With a serrated knife, slice a

1-inch-thick layer from the top of the cake and set aside. Cut the center out of the cake, leaving a 1-inch-thick wall on all sides.

7. With the mixer on medium speed, beat the filling until stiff peaks form. Do not overbeat. Cut half of the cake removed from the center into ½-inch cubes to make 5 cups. Fold the cake cubes into the filling and spoon into the hollow of the cake. (Any remaining cake scraps can be used for snacking.)

8. Invert the reserved cake slice onto the work surface with the cut side up; spread with raspberry preserves. Place the cake slice, preserves side down, on the filled cake. Cover the cake lightly and refrigerate several hours or overnight before serving.

INTO THE FOLD

Gently incorporating a light and airy mixture like beaten egg whites or whipped cream into either a thicker batter or a dry flour-sugar mixture demands careful but not obsessive attention. The goal is simply to blend the two mixtures without losing any of the air bubbles from the egg whites or the whipped cream. Some bakers fold using a hand-held electric mixer on its lowest speed, which you may want to try. We suggest, however, the old-fashioned spatula-in-hand method.

When folding egg whites or whipped cream into a batter, as in our Bunt Cake, page 16, add the lighter mixture to the batter and with a rubber spatula cut down through the center of the batter to the bottom of the bowl. Turn the spatula and bring it up alongside the bowl. Do this slowly three or four times, turning the bowl each time until the two mixtures are just blended and there are no visible streaks of egg whites or cream. When folding dry ingredients into beaten egg whites, fold the dry into the whites one third at a time until just blended.

After folding, move quickly to pour the batter into the prepared pans and bake.

Lime Chiffon Cake

Using vegetable oil instead of butter or shortening was for years the well-guarded secret to chiffon cake's light and airy texture. It remained a secret until Harry Baker, a baker oddly enough, gave Betty Crocker the formula. The big cake company then took the recipe and made chiffon the fad cake of the 1940s. This cake is very much like the Hollywood Brown Derby's famous moist Grapefruit Cake but with the light, sweeter tang of lime.

MAKES 12 SERVINGS

2¼ cups sifted cake flour
1¼ cups granulated sugar
1 tablespoon baking powder
¼ teaspoon salt
4 egg yolks
½ cup vegetable oil
½ cup water
¼ cup lime juice
1 tablespoon finely grated
* lime rind*
8 egg whites, at room
* temperature*

½ teaspoon cream of tartar

Lime Frosting:
1 cup confectioners' sugar
2 teaspoons fresh lime juice
1 drop green food coloring

Candied Lime Peel
* (optional):*
2 limes
½ cup granulated sugar
¼ cup boiling water

1. Heat the oven to 325°F. In a medium-size bowl, combine the flour, 1¼ cups granulated sugar, baking powder, and salt. Make a well in the center of the flour mixture and add, in order, the egg yolks, oil, water, lime juice, and lime rind. With an electric mixer on medium speed, beat the mixture until smooth.

2. In a large bowl, combine the egg whites and cream of tartar. With clean beaters and the mixer on high speed, beat the egg whites until very stiff peaks form. Very gently fold the lime batter into the egg whites until just combined. Pour the mixture into an ungreased 10-inch tube pan.

3. Bake the cake 65 to 70 minutes, or until a cake tester inserted in the center comes out clean. Invert the pan over a bottle. Cool the cake completely in the pan, about 1 hour.

4. Prepare the Lime Frosting: In a small bowl, mix the confectioners' sugar, lime juice, and food coloring until smooth. Set aside.

5. If desired, prepare the Candied Lime Peel: Carefully peel the limes in a long spiral. Scrape any white membrane from the back of the peel. Trim the peel into ¼-inch-wide strips, leaving them as long as possible. In a small saucepan, combine the ½ cup granulated sugar and boiling water over medium heat. Add the lime peel, several strips at a time; simmer 1 minute until the peel is glazed. With a fork, remove the peel to a piece of waxed paper to cool.

6. When the cake is cool, with a knife, carefully loosen the edge of the cake, invert the pan onto a serving plate and unmold the cake. Spread the top of the cake with the lime frosting, allowing some of the frosting to run down the side. If desired, place the candied lime peel on the top of the cake.

EGG WHITES

Producing perfectly beaten egg whites, the kind that are stiff and moist sculptures of light peaks, seems to be a matter of timing and technique.

Timing: It takes about two minutes to beat two room-temperature egg whites into stiff peaks that are neither too dry nor too wet but with just enough moisture to allow them to sit firm in the bowl even when the bowl is gently swirled.

Technique: It takes a large bowl — not aluminum (because it tends to tint the whites a blue/gray) or plastic (because it may have traces of grease that would break the whites down) — and a large balloon whisk or the whip of an electric mixer to beat enough air into the whites to make them increase so much in volume. It also takes steadfastness — once you've begun beating, don't stop until the whites are firm and form stiff peaks. If your egg whites suffer from your overzealousness, they may end up dry, broken down, and rubbery.

Overbeaten whites are not a failed cause. Beat one unbeaten white into three or four overbeaten ones for about 30 seconds and they will usually revive.

Chocolate Cream Roll

Light and spongy thin cakes rolled around cream fillings have been popular ever since the English and French introduced them to our American dessert table. When rolling the cake, handle it gently to avoid tears and holes. If there are snags on the final rolled surface, cover them with a dusting of confectioners' sugar.

MAKES 8 SERVINGS

4 1-ounce squares semisweet chocolate
4 eggs, separated, at room temperature
⅓ cup granulated sugar
¾ teaspoon vanilla extract
⅓ cup water

½ cup all-purpose flour
1 teaspoon baking soda

Cream Filling:
1 cup (½ pint) heavy cream
3 tablespoons coffee-flavored liqueur

Confectioners' sugar

1. Heat the oven to 375°F. Lightly grease a 15½- by 10½-inch jelly-roll pan. Line the bottom with waxed paper; grease and flour the waxed paper. In a 1-quart saucepan, heat the chocolate over low heat until the chocolate melts and is smooth; set aside.

2. In a small bowl, with an electric mixer on high speed, beat the egg yolks, granulated sugar, and vanilla until the mixture is very thick and lemon colored, about 5 minutes. Reduce the mixer speed to low, and beat in the chocolate and water. Beat the flour and baking soda into the chocolate mixture until well combined.

3. In a large bowl, with clean beaters and the mixer on high speed, beat the egg whites until stiff peaks form. Fold the chocolate batter into the egg whites. Spread the batter evenly in the prepared pan.

4. Bake the cake 15 minutes, or until the center springs back when lightly pressed with a fingertip. Cool the cake in the pan on a wire rack for 10 minutes. Meanwhile, sprinkle a cloth towel with 2 tablespoons confectioners' sugar. Invert the pan, and unmold the cake onto the prepared towel. Remove the waxed paper, and trim all the crisp edges off

the cake. Starting from one of the short ends, roll up the cake in the towel. Place the cake, seam side down, on the rack to cool completely.

5. Prepare the Cream Filling: In a small bowl, with the mixer on medium speed, beat the cream, 2 tablespoons confectioners' sugar, and 1 tablespoon liqueur until stiff peaks form.

6. Unroll the cooled cake and sprinkle with the remaining 2 tablespoons liqueur. Spread with the whipped cream mixture and reroll the cake without the towel. Place the cake, seam side down, on a serving plate. Cover and refrigerate until ready to serve. Sift confectioners' sugar over the cake before serving.

BAKING POWDER

Invented in 1856, baking powder is the chemical leavener that helped to change the texture of American cakes from buttery dense to light and moist. It is a mixture of baking soda and cream of tartar (a phosphate salt). When the powder is added to a liquid such as cake batter and subjected to heat, it produces bubbles of carbon dioxide, which make the batter rise into a cake.

In the early days, baking powder was single-acting. That means that as soon as the powder and liquid came together, the bubbling reaction took place all at once. A baker had to mix the batter and get it in the oven quickly in order to get the best results from the rising action of the leavener. Most brands sold in this country nowadays are double-acting, meaning that in a time-released way, carbon dioxide is first produced when the powder is added to the butter. Then more carbon dioxide is produced during baking.

Baking powder is sold in an airtight can to ensure freshness and potency. To test for freshness, add 1 teaspoonful to ½ cup hot water. If you see vigorous bubbling, your baking powder is still active.

Marbled Mocha Angel Food Cake

············

A ngel food cake is named for its fluffy, light-as-a-cloud texture and sweet taste. It differs from chiffon cake in that it is made with no fat or egg yolks and it rises high only because of egg whites. For grown-up tastes, this angel food cake is marbled with chocolate and espresso coffee. Serve it with fresh raspberries and mint sprigs.

MAKES 10 SERVINGS

1¼ cups all-purpose flour	3 tablespoons cocoa powder
1¼ cups sugar	1 half-pint basket (1 cup)
¼ teaspoon salt	raspberries for garnish
12 egg whites, at room	(optional)
temperature	10 sprigs fresh mint for
½ teaspoon cream of tartar	garnish (optional)
2 teaspoons instant espresso	
powder	

1. In a medium-size bowl, combine the flour, ½ cup sugar, and the salt. Heat the oven to 350°F. In a large bowl, with an electric mixer on high speed, beat the egg whites and cream of tartar until frothy. Gradually add the remaining ¾ cup sugar and continue beating until stiff peaks form.

2. Gently fold the flour mixture into the egg white mixture. Pour two thirds of the batter into an ungreased 10-inch tube pan. Divide the remaining batter between 2 small bowls. Stir the espresso into one bowl and 2 tablespoons cocoa into the other just until combined. Spoon both batters randomly into the batter in the pan and lightly cut with a knife to marbleize.

3. Bake the cake 35 to 40 minutes, or until a cake tester inserted in the center comes out clean. Invert the pan over a bottle. Cool the cake completely in the pan, about 1 hour. With a knife, loosen the edge of the cake, invert the pan onto a serving plate, and unmold the cake.

4. To serve, cut the cake into wedges. Sift the remaining 1 table-spoon cocoa over the tops of the wedges, and, if desired, garnish with raspberries and mint sprigs.

Plaid Ribbon Cake, page 82

Calico Spice Cake, page 80

Yellow Jelly-Roll Cake

············

This is the American classic. Made and sold for years in every soda fountain in the country, it's rarely seen in cake keepers nowadays. Serve it as a snack with coffee or as lunchtime dessert. Fill the roll with any jelly you like. Be sure to use a serrated knife for cutting slices for serving.

MAKES 8 SERVINGS

1 cup sifted cake flour	1 teaspoon grated lemon rind
1 teaspoon baking powder	½ teaspoon vanilla extract
¼ teaspoon salt	1 cup strawberry or red
4 eggs, at room temperature	currant jelly
⅔ cup granulated sugar	
¼ cup water	Confectioners' sugar

1. Heat the oven to 375°F. Lightly grease a 15½- by 10½-inch jelly-roll pan. Line the bottom with waxed paper; grease and flour the paper. Into a small bowl, sift the flour, baking powder, and salt.

2. In a large bowl, with an electric mixer on high speed, beat the eggs until fluffy and thickened. Gradually add the granulated sugar, beating constantly, until the mixture is very thick and lemon colored, about 5 minutes. Reduce the mixer speed to low, and beat in the water, lemon rind, and vanilla. Gently fold in the flour mixture. Spread the batter in the prepared pan.

3. Bake the cake 12 to 15 minutes, or until the center springs back when lightly pressed with fingertip. Cool the cake in the pan on a wire rack for 10 minutes. Meanwhile, sprinkle a cloth towel with confectioners' sugar. Invert the cake onto the prepared towel, remove the waxed paper, and trim all the crisp edges off the cake. Starting from one of the short edges, roll up the cake in the towel. Place the cake, seam side down, on the rack to cool completely.

4. Unroll the cake and spread the jelly over the surface. Reroll the cake without the towel. Place the cake, seam side down, on a serving plate. Sift confectioners' sugar over the cake before serving.

Fantastic Chokahlúa Cheesecake

If chocolate cheesecake isn't chocolatey enough for you, try this triple threat. Chocolate crust, bittersweet filling, and a dark chocolate topping flavored with coffee liqueur come together to make this a truly fantastic dessert.

MAKES 12 SERVINGS

Chocolate-Wafer Crust:
¼ cup (½ stick) unsalted
    butter
1⅓ cups chocolate-wafer
    crumbs (26 or 27 wafers)
1 tablespoon sugar

Chocolate-Cream Cheese
    Filling:
1½ cups (9 ounces)
    semisweet chocolate chips
2 tablespoons unsalted butter
¼ cup coffee-flavored liqueur

2 8-ounce packages cream
    cheese, softened
2 eggs
⅓ cup sugar
¼ teaspoon salt
1 cup (½ pint) sour cream

Chocolate Topping:
¼ cup semisweet chocolate
    chips
1 tablespoon coffee-
    flavored liqueur
1 tablespoon light corn syrup
1 cup (½ pint) sour cream

1. Prepare the Chocolate-Wafer Crust: In a 1-quart saucepan, melt the butter over low heat. Remove from the heat; stir in the crumbs and 1 tablespoon sugar. Press the mixture into the bottom of a 9-inch springform pan; set aside. Heat the oven to 350°F.

2. Prepare the Chocolate-Cream Cheese Filling: In a 2-quart saucepan, heat the chocolate, butter, and liqueur over low heat, stirring constantly, until smooth. Remove the chocolate mixture from the heat and cool slightly.

3. In a large bowl, with an electric mixer on medium speed, beat the cream cheese until smooth and fluffy. Add the eggs, one at a time, beating well after each addition. Beat in the ⅓ cup sugar, salt, and sour cream. Gradually beat in the chocolate mixture. Pour the filling into the prepared crust.

4. Bake the cheesecake 1 hour, or until the filling is barely set in the center. Turn off the oven, and let the cheesecake remain there 1 hour longer. Remove the cheesecake from the oven, and cool in the pan on a wire rack. Cover and refrigerate until well chilled, at least 4 hours.

5. Before serving, prepare the Chocolate Topping: In a 1-quart saucepan, heat the chocolate, liqueur, and corn syrup over low heat, stirring constantly until smooth, about 3 minutes. Remove the chocolate mixture from the heat and cool to room temperature.

6. Make a decorating bag from a piece of waxed paper or plastic sandwich bag; spoon the chocolate mixture into the bag. Cut off the tip or corner to make a tiny opening. Remove the side of the pan from the cheesecake. Place the cheesecake on a serving plate. Spread the top with sour cream, and pipe chocolate "trees" to decorate the cheesecake. If preferred, drizzle the chocolate mixture over the top.

QUICK FINISHES

Sometimes all you need for a quick and sweet decorative finish for a plain cake or cupcakes is your microwave oven and a few ingredients from your pantry.

For a speedy, rich chocolate glaze, combine ¾ cup (about 4 ounces) semisweet chocolate chips, ¼ cup cream, and and 1 tablespoon vanilla extract or orange-flavored liqueur in a 1-quart glass bowl. Cover loosely with waxed paper and microwave on medium for 30 seconds. Stir and microwave 2 minutes more, stirring every so often. Remove the bowl from the microwave and beat the glaze with a spoon until it's smooth. Spoon over plain cakes, angel foods, or cupcakes.

A quick citrus glaze can be made without the help of the microwave. Combine ½ cup confectioners' sugar, 2 tablespoons lemon, orange, or lime juice, and ½ teaspoon vanilla extract in a bowl. Stir until smooth and spoon over warm cakes or cupcakes. Sprinkle with finely chopped almonds or shredded coconut.

Passionfruit Cheesecake

············

Here is a wonderful dessert to make for the one you love. Even though passionfruit is not a noted aphrodisiac, it seems to become one when combined here with cream cheese and grenadine. The secret to tropical sweet cake is the ripeness of the fruit. Look for a fruit 3 inches long with a dark purple and dimpled skin. The fruit should feel firm and heavy.

MAKES 10 SERVINGS

2 8-ounce packages low-fat
   cream cheese, softened
1 15-ounce container
   part-skim ricotta cheese
⅓ cup sugar
4 eggs whites
2 very ripe passionfruits
2 teaspoons grenadine syrup,
   or 4 to 6 drops red food
   coloring
1 teaspoon bitters

Passionfruit Glaze:
2 passionfruits
¾ cup water
1 tablespoon sugar
1 tablespoon cornstarch
1 teaspoon grenadine syrup,
   or several drops red food
   coloring
½ teaspoon bitters

1. Heat the oven to 300°F. Grease a 9-inch springform pan or a 9-inch heart-shaped pan. For the heart-shaped pan, cut four 18- by 2-inch strips of heavy-duty aluminum foil. Place the strips, 2 in each direction, in the bottom of the pan, with the ends extending up the side and over the edge of the pan; grease the strips. (These strips will be used to help remove the cheesecake from the pan after baking.)

2. In a large bowl, with an electric mixer on medium speed, beat the cream cheese and ricotta until smooth and fluffy. Beat in the sugar. Add the egg whites, one at a time, beating well after each addition.

3. Cut the very ripe passionfruit in half. Place a fine mesh strainer over a cup, and scrape the pulp and squeeze the juice and seeds of the fruits into the strainer. With a spoon, press as much of the passionfruit pulp as possible through the strainer; discard the seeds. Add the passionfruit juice and pulp, 2 teaspoons grenadine syrup, and 1 teaspoon bitters to the cheese mixture. With the mixer on medium speed, beat until well combined. Spoon the cheese mixture into the prepared pan.

4. Bake the cheesecake 45 to 50 minutes, or until the center is just set. Remove the cheesecake from the oven, and immediately run a spatula around the edge to loosen. Cool the cheesecake completely on a wire rack. Cover and refrigerate the cheesecake at least 4 hours, or overnight.

5. To serve, remove the side of the springform pan, and place the cheesecake on a serving plate. For the heart-shaped pan, warm the bottom of the pan by dipping it in a shallow pan of hot water. Holding the strips of foil, carefully lift the cheesecake onto a serving plate; pull the foil to remove it from under the cheesecake.

6. Prepare the Passionfruit Glaze: Cut the passionfruit in half. Into a 1-quart saucepan, scrape the pulp and squeeze the juice and seeds of the fruits. Add the water, sugar, cornstarch, 1 teaspoon grenadine syrup, and ½ teaspoon bitters. Heat the mixture to boiling, stirring constantly. Cook the mixture until it is thick and translucent, about 1 minute. Spoon the glaze over the cheesecake, allowing some to run over the edge. Serve the cheesecake immediately, or refrigerate until ready to serve.

MAKING TWO LAYERS FROM ONE

When you cut a cake into even layers, a couple of reliable techniques work. One is the eyeball method, where you judge by sight where the middle surface of the layer is. Be sure to place the cake on a surface that allows you to rotate it easily. (A turntable or waxed paper placed on a smooth surface are both good for this.) Use a 10-inch serrated knife and hold the blade steady against the side of the layer where you intend to cut. Place the palm of your other hand on top of the cake and rotate the cake slowly until there is a shallow groove all around the side of the cake. To slice the layer, begin a gentle sawing motion on the groove line and continue rotating the cake until it is sliced all the way through.

The second technique allows you to measure first. With a ruler, measure up from the base of the cake and mark the halfway spot on the layer by inserting a toothpick into the cake. Do this every 2 inches and when you slice, follow the toothpick marks.

Cocoa Cake

Complete with a "Happy Birthday" message piped in blue royal frosting, this is the cake for celebration and surprise. Three cocoa layers filled and swirled with creamy white frosting produce a cake to sing over. Allow two days to make the cake and decorations. A pastry bag with a small star tip is a must.

MAKES 10 SERVINGS

Royal Frosting:
1 cup confectioners' sugar
1 egg white
⅛ teaspoon cream of tartar
Blue liquid food coloring

1 cup (2 sticks) butter,
softened
1¾ cups granulated sugar
1 tablespoon vanilla extract
3 eggs
2¼ cups cake flour

1 cup cocoa powder
1½ teaspoons baking
powder
1 teaspoon baking soda
¼ teaspoon salt
1¾ cups milk

Seven-Minute Frosting
(page 24)
3- to 3½-inch blue candles
(optional)

1. Prepare the Royal Frosting: On a piece of paper, print the message in ¾-inch block letters. Tape the paper onto a baking sheet. Tape a piece of waxed paper over the letters. In a small bowl, with an electric mixer on low speed, beat the confectioners' sugar, egg white, and cream of tartar until combined. Increase the mixer speed to high, and beat the frosting until thick and fluffy. Tint the frosting with one or two drops of blue food coloring. Spoon the frosting into a pastry bag fitted with a small star tip. Pipe a thin, flat line of frosting over each letter. Then pipe small stars on top of each letter to completely cover the line. If desired, make extra letters in case of breakage. Set aside overnight, uncovered, to dry.

2. Heat the oven to 350°F. Grease and flour three 9-inch round baking pans. In a large bowl, with the mixer on medium speed, beat the butter, granulated sugar, and vanilla until light and fluffy. Add the eggs, one at a time, beating well after each addition.

3. Into a medium-size bowl, sift the flour, cocoa, baking powder, baking soda, and salt. With the mixer on low speed, and beginning and ending with the flour mixture, alternately beat the flour mixture and the milk into the butter mixture, until well combined. Divide the batter among the prepared pans.

4. Bake the cakes 25 to 30 minutes, or until a cake tester inserted in the center comes out clean. Cool the cakes in the pans on wire racks for 10 minutes. Remove the cakes from the pans and cool completely on the racks.

5. Prepare the Seven-Minute Frosting: Follow the instructions but substitute water for the coconut liquid and vanilla extract for the coconut flavoring.

6. To assemble the cake, place one cake layer on a serving plate. Spread the top with ½ cup frosting. Place a second cake layer on top of the first, and spread the top with ½ cup frosting. Top with the remaining cake layer. Spread the top and side of the cake with the remaining frosting. Lift the letters off the waxed paper with a knife, and arrange the message and the candles on top of the cake.

KEEPING THE CAKE: FREEZING

Be sure to cool an unfrosted cake completely before freezing it. Wrap it tightly in plastic wrap, then again in aluminum foil or heavy-duty freezer wrap and it will keep several months. Cakes finished with most buttercream frostings can be frozen, too. Place the cake in the freezer long enough to freeze the frosting so that it is very firm. Remove the cake and wrap it in plastic wrap, then again in aluminum foil. Try to make it as airtight as possible. Return the cake to the freezer, where it will keep odor-free and moisture-free for several months. To thaw a frosted cake, unwrap it and let it thaw in the refrigerator overnight. An unfrosted cake can thaw at room temperature in its wrapper in about 2 hours.

Calico Spice Cake

PHOTOGRAPH ON PAGE 72

Sugar and spice and one of our prettiest special occasion cakes! Choose edible flowers for decoration. They should be fresh from a non-toxic (no sprays) garden. Roses, daisies, violets, geraniums, lilacs, and pansies are all delicious. Never decorate with or eat flowers from a florist. And be wary of sparklers that leave a sooty residue as they burn. Test them first before decorating the cake. If yours are the sooty sort, insert them into the cake at an angle extending away from the cake, so the residue falls beside the cake.

MAKES 10 SERVINGS

¾ cup (1½ sticks) butter or margarine, softened
2¼ cups firmly packed light-brown sugar
2 teaspoons vanilla extract
3 eggs
3¾ cups cake flour
1 tablespoon ground cinnamon
1½ teaspoons ground nutmeg
1½ teaspoons baking powder
1½ teaspoons baking soda
1 teaspoon salt
½ teaspoon ground allspice
2 cups buttermilk

Decorator Frosting:
2 1-pound packages confectioners' sugar
1 cup (2 sticks) butter or margarine, softened
Milk
2 teaspoons almond extract
1 3-ounce package cream cheese, softened
Assorted liquid food colorings

Sparklers or candles for decoration (optional)
Nontoxic, edible fresh flowers for decoration (optional)

1. Heat the oven to 350°F. Grease and flour three 9-inch round baking pans. In a large bowl, with an electric mixer on medium speed, beat the butter, brown sugar, and vanilla until light and fluffy. Add the eggs, one at a time, beating well after each addition.

2. Into a medium-size bowl, sift the flour, cinnamon, nutmeg, baking powder, baking soda, salt, and allspice. With the mixer on low speed, and beginning and ending with the flour mixture, alternately beat the flour mixture and the buttermilk into the butter mixture until well combined. Divide the batter among the prepared pans.

3. Bake the cakes 20 to 25 minutes, or until a cake tester inserted in the center comes out clean. Cool the cakes in pans on wire racks for 10 minutes. Remove the cakes from pans and cool completely on racks.

4. Prepare the Decorator Frosting: In a large bowl, with the mixer on low speed, beat the confectioners' sugar, butter, ⅓ cup milk, and the almond extract until combined. Scrape the bowl. Increase the mixer speed to high, and beat the frosting, adding 2 to 3 tablespoons more milk if necessary, until the frosting is light and fluffy. Remove 1 cup frosting to a small bowl; beat in the cream cheese. Remove ½ cup frosting to another small bowl; with red and blue food coloring, tint the frosting violet. Remove ¼ cup frosting to a third small bowl; tint the frosting with green food coloring. With red and yellow food coloring, tint the remaining frosting an apricot color.

5. To assemble the cake, place one cake layer on a serving plate. Spread the top with half the cream cheese frosting. Place a second cake layer on top of the first and spread the top with the remaining cream cheese frosting. Top with the remaining cake layer. Spread the top and side of the cake with the apricot-colored frosting.

6. To decorate the cake, spoon the violet frosting into a medium-size pastry bag fitted with a small drop flower tip. Pipe a border of small flowers along the top edge of the cake. Pipe small flowers to cover the top and side of the cake. Spoon the green frosting into a small pastry bag fitted with a small leaf tip. Pipe 1 or 2 leaves at intervals along the border and beside the flowers on the top and side of the cake. If desired, top the cake with sparklers, and arrange the fresh flowers at the base of the cake on the serving plate.

CUPCAKE TIPS

If there are empty muffin-pan cups when you are baking a batch of cupcakes, fill the empties two thirds full with water. This will make for even baking of the others. Most cupcakes will keep 3 days stored in an airtight container and up to 2 months frozen.

Plaid Ribbon Cake

PHOTOGRAPH ON PAGE 71

This is a delicious almond-flavored cake that is also a brightly wrapped gift box. Although creating the final effect is not difficult, allow yourself plenty of time.

MAKES 10 SERVINGS

3¾ cups cake flour
1½ cups granulated sugar
3½ teaspoons baking
   powder
¾ teaspoon salt
1¾ cups (3½ sticks)
   butter or margarine,
   softened
1½ cups milk
4 eggs
2 teaspoons vanilla extract
1 teaspoon almond extract

Almond Frosting:
1½ 1-pound packages
   confectioners' sugar

⅔ cup vegetable shortening
6 to 7 tablespoons milk
2 teaspoons almond extract
¼ teaspoon salt
¼ cup chopped toasted
   almonds

Plaid Wrapping Decoration:
Heavy cardboard
4 12-inch pieces of string
Assorted liquid food colorings
8-inch matchstick candles
2 16-inch pieces striped or
   plaid ribbons

1. Heat the oven to 350°F. Grease and flour two 9-inch square baking pans. In a large bowl, combine the flour, granulated sugar, baking powder, and salt. Add the butter, milk, eggs, vanilla, and almond extract. With an electric mixer on low speed, beat the batter, scraping the bowl frequently, just until no lumps remain. Divide the batter between the prepared pans and smooth the tops.

2. Bake the cakes 35 to 40 minutes, or until a cake tester inserted in the center comes out clean. Cool the cakes in the pans on wire racks for 10 minutes. Remove the cakes from the pans and cool completely on the racks.

3. Prepare the Almond Frosting: In the large bowl of a heavy-duty electric mixer on low speed, beat the confectioners' sugar, vegetable shortening, milk, almond extract, and salt until combined. Scrape the

bowl. Increase the mixer speed to high, and beat the frosting until light and fluffy. Set aside.

4. Make a 9-inch-square from the cardboard; cover with aluminum foil. To assemble the cake, place one cake layer, upside down, on the foil-covered cardboard. Spread the top with ¼ of the frosting; sprinkle with the toasted almonds. Place the other cake layer, right side up, on top of the first. Spread the top and side of the cake with the remaining frosting.

5. Elevate the cake, placing it on a box or bowl, so that there is at least a 2-inch space between the edge of the cake and the surface of the counter. Put each piece of string in a custard cup with 1 teaspoon water. Add 6 drops food coloring to each cup, so that one string is colored yellow, one red, one green, and one blue.

6. Wearing rubber gloves to protect your hands from the coloring, pull the yellow string tight and lightly touch the top of the cake, making 4 evenly spaced lines in one direction and 4 in the other direction. Redipping the string as necessary, make vertical lines on the side, which extend from the lines on the top of the cake down the side to the base of the cake. Make 2 parallel horizontal lines on the side of the cake, creating a continuous belt. Repeat with the red, green, and blue strings, spacing each to create a plaid pattern.

7. Position the candles in a cluster near one corner of the cake, tilting them out at an angle. Tie the ribbons in bows and place them at the base of the candles.

FINISHING TOUCHES: FLOWERS

Fresh edible flowers are a lovely and inviting finishing touch to any frosted cake. Make sure the flowers have not been subjected to insecticide sprays or dyes. You can arrange sprigs of apple blossoms, peach, orange, or lemon blossoms as a bouquet on top of the cake, or sprinkle rose petals around the bottom as a border. Other edible and decorative flowers are violets, petunias, honeysuckle, lilacs, day lilies, and hibiscus.

Stenciled Star Cake
PHOTOGRAPH ON PAGE 35

Cocoa cream filling between layers of marble cake and an intensely dark smooth frosting make this the cake for the chocolate-loving star in your life. Stenciled stars made of bright-white confectioners' sugar make it particularly festive looking.

MAKES 10 SERVINGS

2 cups granulated sugar
⅔ cup butter or margarine,
   softened
3 eggs
2 teaspoons vanilla extract
3 cups cake flour
2½ teaspoons baking
   powder
½ teaspoon salt
1⅔ cups milk
½ cup cocoa powder
¼ cup water

Cocoa Cream Filling:
½ cup heavy cream
1 tablespoon cocoa powder
1 tablespoon confectioners'
   sugar
½ teaspoon vanilla extract

Chocolate Frosting:
¾ cup evaporated milk
8 1-ounce squares semisweet
   chocolate, chopped
1 teaspoon vanilla extract
Pinch of salt

2 tablespoons confectioners'
   sugar

1. Heat the oven to 350°F. Grease and flour two 9-inch round baking pans. In a large bowl, with an electric mixer on medium speed, beat 1¾ cups granulated sugar and the butter until light and fluffy. Add the eggs, one at a time, beating well after each addition. Beat in the vanilla.

2. In a small bowl, combine the flour, baking powder, and salt. With the mixer on low speed, and beginning and ending with the flour mixture, alternately beat the flour mixture and the milk into the butter mixture until well combined. In the small bowl, combine the remaining ¼ cup granulated sugar and the cocoa. Gradually stir in the water until smooth. Fold 1½ cups batter into the cocoa mixture until smooth. Divide the remaining batter between the prepared pans. Drop the cocoa

batter by tablespoonfuls into the plain batter, dividing it evenly between the two pans. With a fork, swirl the batter to marbleize.

3. Bake the cakes 35 to 40 minutes, or until a cake tester inserted in the center comes out clean. Cool the cakes in the pans on wire racks for 5 minutes. Remove the cakes from the pans and cool on the racks.

4. Prepare the Cocoa Cream Filling: In a small bowl, combine the cream, cocoa, confectioners' sugar, and vanilla. Cover and refrigerate 30 minutes. With the mixer on medium speed, beat the cocoa mixture until stiff peaks form. Set aside.

5. Prepare the Chocolate Frosting: In a 1-quart saucepan, heat the evaporated milk to boiling. Remove from the heat and stir in the chocolate, vanilla, and salt until the chocolate melts. Set aside until the mixture is slightly thickened, about 30 minutes.

6. Place one cake layer on a serving plate. Spread the top with the cocoa cream filling. Place the second cake layer on top of the first. Spread the top and side of the cake with the chocolate frosting. Set aside at least 1 hour, or refrigerate 30 minutes, until the frosting sets.

7. Meanwhile, cut a 9-inch round from waxed paper. Using a star-shaped cookie cutter or a 1-inch star cut from cardboard, trace 7 to 9 stars on the waxed paper round. Cut out the stars, leaving the round intact.

8. Just before serving, place the waxed paper pattern lightly on top of the cake. Sift 2 tablespoons confectioners' sugar over the pattern, filling in the star shapes. Carefully remove the waxed paper.

Equivalents Table

EQUIVALENTS FOR COMMON INGREDIENTS

Granulated sugar ~~~~~~~~~~1 pound ~~~~~~~~~~~~~~~~~~~~~~~~~~~2 cups
Brown sugar ~~~~~~~~~~~~~1 pound ~~~~~~~~~~~~~~~~~~~~~~~~~2¼ cups
Confectioners' sugar ~~~~~~~1 pound ~~~~~~~~~~~~~~~~~~~~~~~~~~~4 cups
Chocolate ~~~~~~~~~~~~~~~~1 ounce ~~~~~~~~~~~~~~~~~~~~~~¼ cup grated
Cocoa powder ~~~~~~~~~~~~1 pound ~~~~~~~~~~~~~~~~~~~~~~~~~~~4 cups
Walnuts, chopped ~~~~~~~~~4 ounces~~~~~~~~~~~~~~~~~~~~~~~~~~~~~¾ cup
Almonds, whole ~~~~~~~~~5⅓ ounces ~~~~~~~~~~~~~~~~~~~~~~~~~~~~1 cup
    Unblanched, slivered ~~~~1 pound ~~~~~~~~~~~~~~~~~~~~~~~~3½ cups
Flour (unsifted) ~~~~~~~~~2½ ounces~~~~~~~~~~~~~~~~~~~~~~~~~~~~½ cup
                3½ ounces~~~~~~~~~~~~~~~~~~~~~~~~~~~~¾ cup
                5 ounces ~~~~~~~~~~~~~~~~~~~~~~~~~~~~~1 cup
Cake flour (unsifted)   1 pound ~~~~~~~~~~~~~~~~~~~~~~~4¾ cups
Butter ~~~~~~~~~~~~~~~~~~½ ounce ~~~~~~~~~~~~1 tablespoon (⅛ stick)
                2 ounces~~~~~~~~~~~~~~4 tablespoons (½ stick)
                4 ounces ~~~~~~~~~~~~~8 tablespoons (1 stick)
Egg whites ~~~~~~~~~~~~~~~8 to 10~~~~~~~~~~~~~~~~~~~~~~~~~~~~~1cup
Cream cheese ~~~~~~~~~~~~3 ounces ~~~~~~~~~~~~~~~~~~~~~6 tablespoons
Heavy cream ~~~~~~~~~~~~~1 cup ~~~~~~~~~~~~~~2 to 2½ cups whipped

MEASURING EQUIVALENTS

3 teaspoons ~~~~~~~~~~~~~~~~~~~~~~~~1 tablespoon
8 tablespoons ~~~~~~~~~~~~~~~~~~~~~~~~~~~~~½ cup
16 tablespoons ~~~~~~~~~~~~~~~~~~~~~~~~~~~~1 cup
4 liquid ounces ~~~~~~~~~~~~~~~~~~~~~~~~~~~½ cup
1 liquid ounce ~~~~~~~~~~~~~~~~~~~~~2 tablespoons
2 cups ~~~~~~~~~~~~~~~~~~~~~~~~~~~~~~~~~1 pint
4 cups~~~~~~~~~~~~~~~~~~~~~~~~~~~~~~~~1 quart
4 quarts~~~~~~~~~~~~~~~~~~~~~~~~~~~~~1 gallon
1 pound ~~~~~~~~~~~~~~~~~~~~~~~~~~~16 ounces

Conversions Table

WEIGHTS

OUNCES & POUNDS	METRIC EQUIVALENTS
¼ ounce	7 grams
⅓ ounce	10 grams
½ ounce	14 grams
1 ounce	28 grams
1¾ ounces	50 grams
2 ounces	57 grams
2⅔ ounces	75 grams
3 ounces	85 grams
3½ ounces	100 grams
4 ounces (¼ pound)	114 grams
6 ounces	170 grams
8 ounces (½ pound)	227 grams
9 ounces	250 grams
16 ounces (1 pound)	464 grams
1.1 pounds	500 grams
2.2 pounds	1,000 grams (1 kilogram)

TEMPERATURES

°F (FAHRENHEIT)	°C (CENTIGRADE OR CELSIUS)
32 (water freezes)	0
108-110 (warm)	42-43
140	60
203 (water simmers)	95
212 (water boils)	100
225 (very slow oven)	107.2
245	120
266	130
300 (slow oven)	149
350 (moderate oven)	177
375	191
400 (hot oven)	205
425	218
450	232
500 (very hot oven)	260

LIQUID MEASURES

tsp.: teaspoon
Tbs.: tablespoon
8 ounces = 1 cup

U.S. SPOONS & CUPS	METRIC EQUIVALENTS	U.S. SPOONS & CUPS	METRIC EQUIVALENTS
1 tsp.	5 milliliters	⅓ cup + 1 Tbs.	1 deciliter (100 milliliters)
2 tsp.	10 milliliters	1 cup	240 milliliters
3 tsp. (1 Tbs.)	15 milliliters	1 cup + 1¼ Tbs.	¼ liter
3⅓ Tbs.	½ deciliter (50 milliliters)	2 cups	480 milliliters
¼ cup	60 milliliters	2 cups + 2½ Tbs.	½ liter
⅓ cup	85 milliliters	4 cups	960 milliliters
		4⅓ cups	1 liter (1,000 milliliters)

Index